Strength For The Journey

Cycle C Sermons for Pentecost Through Proper 16 Based on the Gospel Texts

Dean Feldmeyer

CSS Publishing Company, Inc.
Lima, Ohio

STRENGTH FOR THE JOURNEY

FIRST EDITION

Library of Congress Cataloging-in-Publication Data:

Names: Feldmeyer, Dean, 1951- author. Title: Strength for the journey : Cycle C Sermons for Pentecost through Proper 16 based on the gospel lessons / Dean Feldmeyer. Description: First edition. | Lima, Ohio : CSS Publishing Company, Inc., [2021] Identifiers: LCCN 2021010781 | ISBN 9780788030260 (paperback) | ISBN 9780788030277 (ebook) Subjects: LCSH: Bible. Luke--Sermons. | Common lectionary (1992). Year C. | Pentecost season--Sermons. | Church year sermons. Classification: LCC BS2595.54 .F45 2021 | DDC 252/.64--dc23
LC record available at https://lccn.loc.gov/2021010781

For more information about CSS Publishing Company resources, visit our website at www.csspub.com, email us at csr@csspub.com, or call (800) 241-4056.

e-book:
ISBN-13: 978-0-7880-3027-7
ISBN-10: 0-7880-3027-2

ISBN-13: 978-0-7880-3026-0
ISBN-10: 0-7880-3026-4

DIGITALLY PRINTED

For Mom and Dad

Contents

PREFACE

When I was a kid, every year we would come back to school in the fall, and everyone in the class would be invited to stand for a couple of minutes and share what they did on their summer vacation. And every year, it seemed to me that everyone else did better things than I did.

Billy and his family went to Disneyland. Martha and her family went to Indian Lake. Brad's family went camping in the Smoky Mountains. Janey's family went to the World's Fair. And the Miller twins, who were rich, went to Paris, for crying out loud.

My parents would patiently explain that, even though it may seem that way, everyone but us didn't belong to the swim club, everyone but us didn't have ten-speed bikes, and everyone but us didn't go on extravagant vacations. With five kids and only one income, we just couldn't afford those kinds of things. But, be that as it may, didn't we have a perfectly nice life?

Take our typical family vacation, for instance:

We would put all our luggage in the rooftop carrier of the station wagon (not the air-conditioned station wagon), pack the whole family into it and take off on a road trip — or, what my dad liked to call "a horseshoe vacation," with not one big destination but a whole bunch of little ones which inevitably included visiting and staying a few nights with relatives in southern Indiana, a couple of state parks, and several historical battlefields or homes of long-dead famous people. Our meals would be eaten at diners or truck stops or roadside picnic tables, or sometimes in the car to allay road monotony, there being no fast-food restaurants in those days. Our lodging, when relatives weren't en-route, would be mom and pop motels. Our entertainment in the car would be through-the-window scavenger hunts, license plate bingo, stories read aloud, and sing-alongs.

I would agree with my mother that our vacations were adequate, but privately, I would complain to my dad that, just once, I would like to go to one of those big, fancy, expensive, exciting places everyone else seemed to visit.

That's when my dad shared with me some of his folk wisdom; in this case, a piece of advice that has informed a big part of my life.

"Dean," he said. "A great vacation isn't about a destination. It's about a journey. I bet if you asked all your friends who went to those big places about what they did or saw on the way and the way back, they wouldn't be able to tell you. They were probably so focused on the destination that they missed the journey. That isn't so for us. For us, the journey is the destination."

At the time, I think I probably mumbled something like, "Yeah, okay." Or, "I suppose." It wasn't until I was an adult that I realized just how right my dad was.

We often spend so much of our time and resources focusing on destinations that we forget to take in and remember the journey. We miss the meadow full of sunflowers. We don't see the serial Burma Shave signs or the clever billboards. We ignore the valleys and the vistas. We are so intent on the grade or the degree that we miss the artful language in the novel or the subtle traits of the characters in the play. We are so absorbed in getting our kids into this or that school that our machinations obliterate their childhoods.

We often talk about our "faith journey," but I often find that what we call a journey is really just a race to get to a vacation destination called "heaven." So intent are we on believing the right things, doing the right things, and reading the right things so we can get to our destination, that we fail to take in the journey when, in fact, the journey is the thing.

And, as my dad would tell you, the journey takes planning and preparation, and it takes a great deal of strength (especially if you're going to be crammed into a station wagon with a wife, five kids, and an English Bull Dog with gastro-intestinal issues.)

The sermons herein are summer sermons, to be preached as people prepare for, embark on, and return from their summer vacation journeys and as they continue on their faith journeys.

I hope they bring a little bit of strength and enjoyment to those wanderings.

Grace and Peace,

Dean Feldmeyer

Pentecost Sunday

John 14:8-17, (25-27)

Never Satisfied

> Phillip said to him, "Lord, show us the Father and we will be satisfied." Jesus said to him, "Have I been with you all this time, Phillip, and still you don't know me? Whoever has seen me has seen the Father.
>
> John 14: 8-9

How is Philip like the Rolling Stones? Right! They can't get no satisfaction. Remember those lyrics from the mid '60s? No matter how much they tried, they 'can't get no satisfaction'".

He and the other disciples had been following Jesus around for about three years, watching him heal people and perform miracles, listening to him as he taught and preached, grilling him with questions, and they still weren't satisfied.

They wanted more.

Phillip stepped up for the whole group and put it into words: "Lord, show us the Father and we will be satisfied." Enough of these parables and stories that make us think. We don't want to have to think or interpret or work at this anymore. We want you to just tell us the answers. Put it out there in bold, stark relief. Make it plain, simple, and direct.

This is the first-century, early-church equivalent of that age-old question, "Teacher, will this be on the final exam?"

Just give us the basics — the bare bones answers — the raw data. Just give us the answers to the questions that will be on the final exam.

Give us those and we'll be satisfied.

Except you know he won't. You can almost hear Jesus rolling his eyes.

Satisfaction is, after all, a hard thing to achieve, isn't it?

There is a story about two friends who ran into each other at a coffee shop. One friend noticed the other sitting at a table by the window, looking sad and forlorn, so he brought his coffee over and sat down opposite him.

"Dave," he said, "Why so glum? Is something wrong?"

"Oh," said his friend, Dave. "Three weeks ago, a cousin I was close to died and left me $50,000 in his will."

"I'm so sorry for your loss, brother," said the friend. "But surely fifty thousand unexpected dollars will mitigate your pain at least a little. Is there anything else?"

"Yeah," said Dave. "Two weeks ago, I heard that an old buddy of mine who I hadn't seen for a long time died and left me $200,000 in his will."

"Oh, my gosh," said the friend. "I'm sure that must have been a horrible shock, and you feel terrible since it had been so long since you and your friend had seen each other. But, on the other hand, $200,000. That's a lot of money."

"Yeah, it is."

"So, why so glum? Is there something else?"

"Well, yeah. Last week, my great-uncle died and left me $1,000,000."

"Really? A million dollars? Dave, you're telling me you're a millionaire and, though I'm sure the loss of your great uncle was painful for you, I would think that over a million dollars in the past three weeks would give you some cause for happiness. Why are you sitting here in such misery?"

Dave looked up from his coffee. "Well, those inheritances were nice, of course. But since then, it's been a whole week and nothing!"

We laugh because there's just a little bit of truth in that anecdote, right?

When Jean and I were first married, I worked while she finished nursing school. I was the manager of a retail music store — the kind that sells musical instruments and sheet music, not the kind that sells record albums — and I made $100.00 a week, plus 3% of the gross sales of the store. I thought I was rich.

Then Jean graduated and got her nursing license, and we

decided to both work for a year before I went back to college. We were rolling in money, averaging a total of about $300.00 per week.

We bought a convertible — used, we weren't completely crazy.

We outfitted the convertible with a state-of-the-art eight-track tape player and huge speakers.

We considered getting a better, nicer apartment and another car. We took up golf.

We even thought about putting my education on hold for another year.

There were just so many things that we wanted to buy, so many things that we convinced ourselves that we really needed to own, to try, to experience.

Then the car started having problems and the eight-track player started eating up our tapes.

Our landlord gave me a choice of either being the maintenance superintendent of the apartment building or having my rent increased.

Thankfully, reality settled comfortably on our shoulders, and we realized that we could be satisfied with less so I could go back to school and get my bachelor's degree.

But it wasn't an easy decision to come to.

Our culture bombards us with constant messages telling us that we are crazy to be satisfied. We should be striving for, working for, grabbing, taking, making more, more, more all the time. To be satisfied with what you are and what you have is to be an unmotivated loser.

Several years ago, I was sitting in a coffee shop in a shopping mall during the Christmas season. I was at a regular table, pretending to read a book on my Kindle, but I couldn't help overhearing a conversation going on at the table, one with higher stools, across the aisle from me.

Two women were seated there, across from each other. Both were youngish — mid-twenties, say — and beautifully dressed and quaffed. They had nametags on their lapels, identifying them as employees of one of the stores in the mall.

So taken was I by what I observed going on at their table, I later wrote a poem about it. I called it:

LUCKY HER

She's pregnant,
Sipping on a milkshake,
Luxuriating in the silky smoothness of the ice cream,

The sweet, rich taste of the chocolate on the back of her tongue,
While under the table
Her hand gently strokes
Her belly.

Meanwhile, her boss,
Thin and pert and
Perfectly quaffed,
Sent down from corporate to fix things,
Nibbles at her salad and
Frets over a ledger:
Sales figures, and
Inventories, and
Work schedules.
That kinda of stuff.
Our soon-to-be mother listens
And takes another sip
off her milkshake,
Tries to look concerned.
But under the table,
Her hand
Is stroking her belly, and
If you look at her eyes, you can see that
She just can't bring herself
To care about ledgers with
Sales figures, and
Inventories, and
Work schedules, and

That kinda of stuff.

I swear, I wanted to jump up and shake her hand and say, good for you, young lady. You know what is important, really important in this life.

But I doubted that her boss would have appreciated my doing that. In fact, I seem to recall her using the phrase, "lack of urgency," with a certain impatience in her voice, like she understood as well as I did that, right now, this girl's priorities did not include sales figures, inventories, work schedules, and stuff.

She had found a satisfaction in something else that no sales figures, no matter how good they were, could ever match for her.

But that is not the way the world wants us to think. We need only read a couple of billboards, watch a couple of commercials, or glance at a couple of ads on our Facebook pages.

The world wants us to be constantly unsatisfied, constantly in search of more and better.

John D. Rockefeller was an oil tycoon and one of America's first millionaires at a time when the average American earned eight to ten dollars per week. It is told that someone once asked him how much money was enough. He answered, "One more dollar."

Money is easier to come by than satisfaction, it seems.

But it's not just money or possessions we're supposed to be unsatisfied with.

When I was a teenager, I didn't have to worry about calories. I was so active that I tended to burn off whatever I ate. And I ate a lot. My friends and I would stop by McDonalds on the way home from a ball game or a date just to grab a snack.

My snacks, in those days, were usually something like a Big Mac, large fries, and a chocolate shake. My friends were the same. And if that was a snack, imagine what my meals were like.

I was a calorie burning machine.

My mother, on the other hand, struggled with her weight most of her adult life, until she went to Weight Watchers and lost nearly 100 pounds. She was such an enthusiastic follower of the

Weight Watcher system that, eventually, she became a lecturer for them and, later, a trainer who trained other lecturers.

We were all very proud of her and, one time, I asked her what the most important thing was that she had learned from Weight Watchers. She told me that, for her, the key was learning to eat, not until you were full, but just until you were satisfied. And then, quit. Leave the table.

Much as I wanted to, I just didn't get it. Satisfied? See, the problem with that for me was that I wasn't satisfied until I was full. For the life of me, I just couldn't see the difference in the two. And as a teenager, I was never really full.

Of course, that isn't the case anymore. Now, as an old man, I get both full and satisfied pretty easily and, usually, right about the same time. With food, that is.

Money, possessions, food, and even ourselves — take your pick. We are expected, even encouraged, to be dissatisfied.

Maybe it's because I'm at the threshold of crossing into my dotage, my senior citizen years, but I'm noticing a lot more commercials on television aimed at convincing seniors that we don't have to be satisfied with who we are.

I never heard of crepe paper skin until I picked up a copy of AARP magazine at the barbershop. I look at those magazine or internet or TV ads with the before and after pictures, for skin cream that removes wrinkles and bags under your eyes and, I'll be honest, I can't tell the difference in the pictures.

Maybe that's because I have old people eyes and should consider some kind of eye surgery, or maybe a facelift, a gastric bypass. Or a Sono Bello procedure, whatever that is. After all, about 18.5 million other Americans had plastic surgeries or procedures last year.

The American Medical Association is not averse to cashing in on our dissatisfaction with our looks. One could do worse, financially speaking, than owning a plastic surgery practice in the US.

Just listen to some of the catch phrases that are used to lure you into a plastic surgery clinic when your level of dissatisfaction with your appearance reaches critical mass:

> "A more beautiful and confident you!"
>
> "A more natural, younger you." (Youth is always a big seller.)
>
> "You can be perfect."
>
> "Because you're precious."
>
> "Boost your confidence." (And probably other things as well.)
>
> "Discover a new you."
>
> "Emerge to incredible possibilities."
>
> "Feel beautiful."
>
> "Helping you achieve your goals." (Well, someone's goals.)
>
> "Holding back the years." (There's that youth thing, again.)
>
> "Improving you."
>
> "Live beautifully."

The world of commerce is counting on you being dissatisfied. But we don't have to cave to that pressure. We can, actually, be satisfied without spending our retirement savings on bigger lips, a tighter face, a boat, a condo with a pool, or a trip to Europe. We can *choose* to be satisfied.

I submit that the road to satisfaction with our lives and ourselves, starts with being satisfied with our relationship with God.

But how? How do we get a spiritual life that is, ultimately, satisfying?

Some people believe that a satisfying spiritual life is to be found in books and lecture halls.

When I was in seminary, I knew people who were there not because they wanted to be pastors or theologians, but because they wanted to find God.

They were always disappointed when the professors told them that they were doing it backwards. Most people usually go to seminary *after* they've found God. Seminary is where you learn how to talk about the God you've found (Theology = *theos* (God) *logos* (words).

Others turn to Christian self-help or what is often referred to as pop theology. There's an author who can prove that God exists in forty thousand, easy to understand, two or three syllable words. No need for faith when this author can give you proof.

There's another who cannot only give you faith, but make you rich at the same time, or at least tell you why you're not rich, which is usually because you don't have the right kind of relationship with God.

And there's another who will heal you of whatever ails you — mental, spiritual, physical, or financial — if you will just say the magic words: "Jesus Christ, my personal Lord and Savior," and become a sustaining member of his ministry with a check every month.

Of course, that's not what Jesus said.

Read today's text and we hear that Jesus said, clearly and without confusion, in small, mostly one and two syllable words, that the path to knowing God, not just knowing *about* God, but having a satisfying relationship with God is to be found in none other than Jesus himself.

"Whoever has seen me has seen the Father."

Do you want to know God? Know Jesus.

Know Jesus, know God.

And according to our Christian tradition, there are two ways to get to know Jesus.

One is through the New Testament, especially the gospels. It is in the words of the synoptic gospels, Matthew, Mark, and Luke, and the spiritual gospel, John, that we find and become acquainted with Jesus.

It is in those books that we see his miracles, hear his teachings and his commandments, and watch his example. It is in that seeing, that hearing, and that watching that we become his disciples.

It is when we stop simply reading the gospels and start actually studying them and discussing them with others who are on the same journey we are on, that we can adopt his name as our own and call ourselves Christian.

That brings us to the other way we can encounter, hear, watch, learn from, and abide with the Master. That is, when we enter into and become a part of his resurrected body, the church.

It is in the fellowship of believers that we see the active, living, loving, and saving Christ.

It is in the worship service that we hear his words. It is in the classroom that we study his teachings. It is in the mission field that we follow his commandments to love. It is in the sacraments and the music that we feel his presence standing next to us. It is in the shared meals, the handshakes, the hugs, the laughter, the shared space, shared time, and shared lives that are found only in the church that we come face to face with Jesus Christ.

Not every time, not all the time, but sometimes.

Sometimes, when we are wrapped in the fellowship of the church, when we are with our Christian brothers and sisters in worship, in song, in service, in prayer, in work and in play, sometimes, at times like those, we look up and realize that we are, really and truly, living and leaning on Jesus, our Lord.

And when we are leaning on him, we are leaning on God the Father, almighty.

A most satisfying state of affairs, to be sure. Amen.

Trinity Sunday

John 16:12-15

Strength For The Journey

> When the Spirit of truth comes, he will guide you into all the truth; for he will not speak on his own, but will speak whatever he hears, and he will declare to you the things that are to come. He will glorify me, because he will take what is mine and declare it to you.
> John 16:13-14

Today is Trinity Sunday. Founded by Pope Pius X in 1911, it is the only feast day on the church calendar that does not celebrate a person or an event, but rather a doctrine, and some say, a reality. Trinity Sunday is celebrated the Sunday after Pentecost, and lasts only one day, which is symbolic of the unity of the Trinity.

It is a day that is given to celebrating and contemplating the Holy Trinity, one of the oldest and most widely accepted of all Christian beliefs and, if you don't mind my saying so, one of the least understood.

Oh, don't look at me. I don't understand it either.

But I have, over the years, done some reading on the subject. Here's a little excerpt from the web site www.prayerist.com:

> "The Trinity is one of the most fascinating — and controversial — Christian teachings. The Trinity is described as a "mystery." By mystery the Church does not mean a riddle, but rather the Trinity is a reality above our human comprehension that we may begin to grasp, but ultimately must know through worship, symbol, and faith. It has been said that mystery is not a wall to run up against, but an ocean in which to swim.

> "Common wisdom is that if you discuss the Trinity for longer than a few minutes, you will slip into heresy, because you are probing the depths of God too deeply...
>
> "Essentially the Trinity is the belief that God is one in essence... but distinct in person... The Greek word for person means "that which stands on its own," or "individual reality," and does not mean the persons of the Trinity are three human beings. Therefore, Christians believe that the Father, the Son, and the Holy Spirit are somehow distinct from one another (not divided though), yet completely united in will and essence."

The article goes on to ask and answer the "How so?" question. How, can this be so?

It offers two illustrations to illustrate how: Our eyes are two distinct "persons", in that they stand distinctly on their own, right? But they are one in will and essence as they produce a single image when we use them to see with.

Or — and, being a musician, I really like this one — "Think of a C-chord. The C, E, and G notes are all distinct notes, but joined together as one chord, the sound is richer and more dynamic than if the notes had been played individually. The notes are all equally important in producing the rich sound, and the sound is lacking and thin if one of the notes is left out."

Whence The Doctrine?

Okay, that's how it works, sort of, but where did it come from?

There is no mention of the Trinity or a Trinity in the Bible. The three persons of the Trinity: Father, Son, and Holy Spirit, are mentioned together only once, and that in the nineteenth verse of chapter 28 of Matthew's gospel. "Go, therefore, and make disciples of all nations, baptizing them in the name of the Father, and of the Son, and of the Holy Spirit."

The doctrine of the Trinity as we know it was formulated in about 400 CE, under the leadership of Saint Basil of Caesarea,

Saint Gregory of Nyssa, and Saint Gregory of Nazianzus. A vague belief or quasi-doctrinal version of God as three-in-one had been floating around since the early church was first formed, but it was under those three that it took, pretty much, the form it has today and that form is accepted in all of the historic confessions of Christianity, even though the impact of the Enlightenment a philosophical/political movement (also known as the Age of Reason, circa. 1715-1789) decreased its importance in some traditions.

Most of us grew up with it as an unquestioned, if little understood, part of our Christian upbringing. We stood and sang the doxology, bearing down on that last line: "Praise Father, Son, and Holy Ghost," as the offering plates were brought solemnly forward by the ushers.

If we had questions about that mysterious formulation, we usually swallowed them for fear that, as was often the case, when you ask preachers a theological question, they tell you "how the watch works" when you really just wanted to know "what time it is."

So, I waded through the doxology and listened to my pastor talk about the Trinity, never really understanding or even trying to understand what we were singing and talking about.

I had no problem with the first part, the Father.

I had always suspected that God was like a father; not just any father, you understand, but sort of a perfect father. Like Atticus Finch, Jim Anderson, Ward Cleaver, Steve Douglas, Andy Taylor, but mostly Atticus Finch.[1] (Some of you may need to do a Google search to find out who those guys are, but people my age knew them well.)

God, the Father was like those guys — kind, patient, understanding, and forgiving. And if he occasionally got it wrong, like in the proposed sacrifice of Isaac, he admitted it and corrected the situation immediately. That's what really good Fathers do, right?

1 The Fathers are, of course, fictional: Atticus Finch *To Kill a Mockingbird*; Jim Anderson "Father Knows Best"; Ward Cleaver "Leave it To Beaver"; Steve Douglas "My Three Sons"; Andy Taylor "The Andy Griffith Show".

And, if you spend enough time with your father, you can actually develop a relationship with him. Even the quiet, introspective, recalcitrant kinds of fathers can be warmed up if we work hard at it.

The son part of the Trinity was no more difficult to figure out than the Father part. The Son is Jesus, right? And where do we find Jesus? Why, in the gospels, of course. You want to know the second person of the Trinity, read the synoptic gospels, Matthew, Mark, and Luke, and then read the spiritual gospel, John.

That will give you a pretty good understanding of just who Jesus was. If you are willing to spend the time and energy, you can develop a close, personal relationship with him.

But the Holy Spirit was and is a hard concept for me to get my mind around. Not to put too fine a point on it, it has been a raspberry seed in my wisdom tooth for most of my thinking and reasoning life, especially when the church insisted upon calling it the Holy Ghost.

Let's stop using that language, okay? I know, it'll be hard to give up the doxology, but in the interest of clarity and modernity, let's make do. The phrase "Holy Ghost" is based on one, not very good, translation of the Greek word *pneuma,* which can be translated spirit, wit, ghost, esprit, or humor, depending on the context. To insist on translating it as "ghost" is counterindicated and, well, just perverse. It smacks of archaic myth and superstition.

It is no wonder that people tend to treat the Holy Spirit as though it is a ghost that hovers just over our shoulder, whispering in our ear, directing our every thought, action, and feeling. Christian theology that has developed over the past 2,000 years, however, tells us there's a whole lot more to it than that.

So, no more talk of "ghosts" in church, okay?

Let's go with the more correct and appropriate translation, "Spirit." In this case, we are talking about a holy spirit, indeed, *the* Holy Spirit.

So, how shall we speak of this Holy Spirit?

Talk About Spirit

Let us speak first of spirits in general, those of the not-so-holy kind.

No, no I'm not speaking of ghosts or haunts. I thought we left that behind. Please, try to keep up.

Rather, I'm speaking of the spirits we speak of and accept as not just harmless but benevolent, even good on a near daily basis — spirit in the common, everyday sense.

The *Cambridge Dictionary* tells us that spirit is a particular way of thinking, feeling, or behaving, especially a way that is typical of a particular group of people, an activity, a time, or a place. The spirit of England, say. If you have it, you have a particular way of behaving, of talking, and of approaching life. You enjoy certain things and eschew others. You probably eat and enjoy bangers and mash, or steak and kidney pie. You call French fries, chips. And you celebrate Boxing Day on the day after Christmas.

Or, for example, there's the spirit of adventure. If you have it, you enjoy risks and the exploration of new and novel things. You go on safaris, you climb mountains, you try things just to see if you can do them. You keep your spouse in a constant state of worry and anxiety.

Or, one more, the Spirit of '76. We've all seen that old painting by Ohio painter Archibald Willard. It depicts a young boy and an old man marching along, playing drums while another man, a wounded soldier, marches with them playing a fife. In the foreground, a wounded soldier lies propped up on a broken caisson wheel, waving his cap while, in the background, other soldiers rally behind the musicians with bayonets fixed.

Commissioned for the American Centennial Exposition of 1875, it was originally titled "Yankee Doodle" but quickly became known as "The Spirit of '76" because people believed that it embodied a specific kind of spirit that was unique to the American people.[2]

Thomas Jewett wrote that at the time of the American Revolution, there was "an intangible something that is known as the 'Spirit of '76.' This spirit was personified by the beliefs and

2 The original painting measures 8'X10' and currently resides in Abbot Hall, the Town Hall of Marblehead, Massachusetts.

actions of that almost mythical group known as the Founding Fathers and is perhaps best exemplified by Thomas Jefferson." Jefferson and the Second Continental Congress believed the Spirit of '76 "included the 'self-evident' truths of being 'created equal' and being 'endowed by their Creator with certain inalienable rights' including life, liberty, and the pursuit of happiness."

That is the Spirit of '76, and I defy you to stand in the national archives and read the original Declaration of Independence without feeling that spirit run up and down your spine and cover you with goose bumps.

The *Merriam-Webster Dictionary* offers this among several definitions of spirit: an animating or vital principle held to give life to physical organisms. That's close to what we're talking about, here.

But my favorite definition is found in, of all places, Wikipedia. It defines "spirit" thus: In folk belief, spirit is the vital principle or animating force within all living things.

Oh, I like that so-called, "folk belief."

Let's hear it again: The vital principle or animating force within all living things. In other words, spirit is what gives a thing life.

Let me try an example:

Animating Principle

Our son, Ben, played in the Ohio State University Marching Band. That's a pretty big deal in Ohio. It is an elite organization with traditions that go back 142 years. It has 110 members, all brass and percussion. The tryouts go for three days every summer, and they are grueling.

When he made it, we were thrilled and determined to see him march at the first home game of the season. Each member of the band gets one free ticket, so he gave us his and another band member who was from out of state sold us his at a reasonable price.

On game days, the band performs a concert of the music they will play at half-time plus a few other songs at St. John's Arena, the 17,276-seat coliseum where the basketball team used to play.

It's called the "best free show in town" and the arena fills up early.

We got there over an hour before starting time for the "skull session" as it's called, found some seats that weren't too bad, and sat down to wait.

A half hour before the show was scheduled to begin, every seat was taken, but there was a decided lack of excitement in the crowd. People were reading the newspaper, eating breakfasts they had brought along, talking, laughing, dozing, and staring into space with blank expressions. Hardly what you'd call animated.

Then, a small group of people near the tunnel entrance began to clap their hands in a three-clap rhythm — clap, clap, clap — clap, clap, clap — over and over. Others took up the cadence until everyone, all 17,276+ were clapping. People began to whistle. Then some began to cheer. And, then we heard it: the drums.

Low at first as the band made it across the campus, and louder and louder until they were in the tunnel then, suddenly, quiet — about eight beats of silence — then a four count on a drum and here they came at a double time march, eight abreast, shoulder to shoulder, heads down, left arm swinging up to chest and back down, around the perimeter of the gym floor until they are all in.

The noise was deafening, people were cheering and whistling, mothers and girlfriends and, okay, a few dads were crying.

Upon reflection, after a few skull sessions, I realized that it wasn't the band alone that animated the crowd on those Saturday mornings. The band brought with it, into the coliseum a certain spirit, a spirit of pride, of tradition, of discipline and skill and art and dedication that overflowed from the members and into the fans.

That spirit would show up again in the stadium, before the game, when the band made what they call their "Ramp Entrance," and again, at half-time when the performed the "Script Ohio." And each time the audience would be enthralled and enlivened by its presence.

That's why the Ohio State University Marching Band is considered part of the athletic department of the school. It plays an integral part in providing the spirit of OSU that is so essential and necessary for a team to win.

Spirit is the reliquary of a thing's essence. Spirit is the part of every person and every human system that holds its meaning and purpose and the gives it authentic life.

A salesman might say, "In the spirit of full disclosure, I must tell you that this car you are about to buy has been wrecked, twice."

It is that spirit that motivates and enlivens the salesman's ethical approach to his customers.

A pastor might say, "Let us enter into a spirit of prayer or worship," for, indeed, prayer and worship are those things that give a Christian fellowship its meaning and purpose.

The spirit of Christmas gives life to the Christmas season.

School spirit gives life to the student body.

The spirit of the law gives life to the law that would otherwise just be cold, unfeeling, wooden words.

If we can accept that a spirit is that animating and the vital principle that gives life to not just organisms, but to systems as well, then let us speak now of a certain kind of spirit that gives a certain kind of authentic life to Christian persons and the system that is called the church.

Because we believe that this spirit comes from God, as a gift to us, we who are motivated and enlivened by it refer to it as holy.

It is the Holy Spirit which gives authentic life and vitality to Christian life, individually, and corporately as the church.

Listen to how Paul closed his second letter to the church in Corinth: "The grace of the Lord Jesus Christ, the love of God, and the communion of the Holy Spirit be with all of you." Look closely at the word, communion. It comes from the Latin meaning "one with." The New International Version (NIV) uses the word, "fellowship."

The "fellowship of the Holy Spirit" is that fellowship that is given life and authenticity by God's Holy Spirit. The Holy Spirit is that spirit which enlivens, strengthens, legitimizes, and animates our fellowship as Christians and it is in that fellowship, the church, that we realize its presence in our lives most keenly. And it is by that presence that we receive in fellowship that we are strengthened for our individual journeys.

Strength For The Journey

God is made known to us as Father, as Son, and as Holy Spirit. In each of these aspects we can come to know the essence of God and in all three, together, we come to know the fullness of God.

But it is through the Holy Spirit that we know God as motivator, animator, and authenticator. It is in God that we discover the strength that we need to make the journey of an authentic life.

I have already talked more than a few minutes and maybe, as the old axiom says, I have slipped into heresy for probing the mystery too deeply, but probably not. No one has ever accused me of being too deep.

I prefer to think that we have spent the past few minutes swimming in the ocean that is the doctrine of the Trinity. We have floated, frolicked, had a good time, and maybe we have even been strengthened a little in our faith by this exercise.

I will end this reflection with on quick story:

> There was a young missionary, Father Paul, who lived and worked with a couple of other missionaries, Father Michael and Brother Bartholomew, in a mountainous region of a South American country. They ran a medical clinic for the native peoples whom they loved and who loved them in return.
>
> One day they ran out of one of the drugs that was necessary for the running of their clinic and so they sent Father Paul down the mountain to the city to purchase some more. They also sent two young native men to go with him as guides since the mountainside was crisscrossed with many hundreds of goat tracks and paths that, to a novice, might all look the same and it would be easy to take the wrong one and get lost.

The three young men, Father Paul and his two guides, made their way down the mountain to the city and the young missionary purchased the necessary drugs and was ready to return up the mountain to the clinic, but his guides were nowhere to be found.

Apparently, they had become fascinated with the allure of the city and decided to explore it. Father Paul could not wait, however. Lives were at stake and the medicine he had purchased was urgently needed.

So, he decided to start back up the mountain without his guides.

It was starting to get dark early, as it does in the mountains, and, as you might expect, Father Paul was soon, hopelessly lost. Eventually, it became dark and he found a small creek with potable water and slept through the night, there. The next morning, he started walking, again, but he could not find the path to the village. Again, he had to sleep on the mountain.

The next morning, he awoke to the sound of people laughing and talking, walked up a path, crested a small rise and there was his village. Father Michael and Brother Bartholomew ran to him and welcomed him home, patting him on the back, relieved that he was well.

He related the story of how his guides had disappeared and the two young men were appropriately chastised by the head-man of the village but everyone wanted to know how he had made it back without guides.

"I prayed," he said.

"Yes, of course," Father Michael said. "You prayed and the Holy Spirit came to you and showed you which path to take. It was a miracle..."

But before he could finish his thought, Father Paul interrupted him. "No, Father, God did answer my prayer, but the Holy Spirit did not show me which path to take. The Spirit gave me the strength to keep trying different paths until I found the one that led me here."

One activity of God's Holy Spirit, maybe the main activity, the primary one, is giving us the strength we need to make the journey we need to make to get us to where God wants us to be. Amen.

Proper 3

Luke 6:39-49

Licensed Fruit Inspectors

Scripture warns us about the pitfalls of passing judgment on others (Matthew 7:1-2 and Luke 6:37-38). God will, we are told, judge us with the same temperament with which we judge our brothers and sisters. But there is a huge difference between establishing ourselves as a moral authority over others, and simply noting choices that people make and the results those choices produce.

Jesus makes this point rather strongly in today's gospel lesson and then pounds it home with a couple of metaphors having to do with eyesight and fruit trees.

"We must not set ourselves up as judges," a mentor of mine used to say, "but we are all licensed fruit inspectors."

WHAT GOES UP

For Want of a Nail
For want of a nail the shoe was lost.
For want of a shoe the horse was lost
For want of a horse the rider was lost.

For want of a rider the message was lost.
For want of a message the battle was lost.
For want of a battle the kingdom was lost.
And all for the want of a horseshoe nail.
(in the public domain)

This old, anonymous proverb reminds us that all acts, even the smallest, most seemingly inconsequential ones, have consequences, often greater than we realize at the time.

For instance: at about 9:30 p.m. on July 1, 2017, thirteen-year-old Noah Inman, of the Chicago suburb of Hammond, Indiana, was playing basketball with some friends and family members when he suddenly fell to the ground. Onlookers thought he was having a seizure so they called an ambulance which took him immediately to the hospital.

Noah never recovered consciousness and died, seven days later in the ICU.

The cause of death was determined to be a bullet which fell from the sky and entered his brain through the top of his head.[3]

Sadly, Noah is not the only example of what police often refer to as "falling bullet" homicide.

A 1994 study from the King/Drew-UCLA Medical Center discovered 118 cases of people killed by falling bullets from 1985-1994. The same study determined that getting shot from the air is extra dangerous. The mortality rate for this type of celebratory gunfire was around 32 %, or over five times higher than that for other types of gunfire because falling bullets frequently strike victims in the head.[4]

The mayor of Hammond, Indiana, reflecting upon Noah Inman's sad death, said that he could not figure out what people are thinking when they shoot guns in the air. Those bullets don't just disappear into the sky, he said. They have to come down somewhere.

What goes up must come down and sometimes with tragic results.

Knowing these things might not put us in a position to judge the moral posture of someone who fires a gun into the air, but it certainly gives us some consequential fruit to inspect: Shooting a gun into the air, not knowing where the bullet is going to come down is a foolish act. And the tree which produces such a foolish act, that is, the human agent, might legitimately be called a foolish tree or, in this case, a foolish person.

Or this....

No one ever says, "I think I'll go out and drink a lot of alcohol and then get in my car and drive out on the highway and kill some

3 https://chicago.cbslocal.com/2017/07/09/13-year-old-boy-struck-by-falling-bullet-in-nw-indiana-dies/
4 https://www.newsweek.com/celebratory-gunfire-new-years-eve-los-angeles-410598

innocent people." But they do it, just the same. They miscalculate how many drinks they've had or they overestimate their ability to function clearly and accurately. They refuse to be convinced by others and, under the influence of drugs or alcohol, they make bad decisions that cost them their lives or the lives of others.

In 2018, the last year for which the figures have been compiled, 10,518 people were killed on America's highways by alcohol impaired drivers and over 200,000 were injured.

Luke told us, in today's gospel lesson, that because we are all guilty, to one degree or another, of occasional bad decisions, we are in no position, morally speaking, to judge the moral standing of someone who makes a poor decision. These numbers, however, are the fruit of the tree called driving under the influence and we are in a perfect position to give that fruit a thorough and thoughtful inspection.

Not all consequences are bad, of course. Good trees tend to produce good fruit.

When our kids were in school, we had a weekend ritual wherein we would visit a little discount shopping mall near our community. The mall had a small food court, a discount movie theater, a comic bookstore, and a used bookstore which gave us all hours of enjoyment.

Generally, on a Sunday afternoon we would go to the mall, browse through the bookstore and the comic book-store and maybe a couple other places and then go to a movie. After the movie we would go to the food court and treat ourselves to an inexpensive dinner.

One evening, while we were eating, the proprietor of one of the little food places came up to our table and asked if it would be okay if he sat down and talked to us for a few minutes. We were surprised by his request, but we felt like we knew this man a little, so often had we eaten at the food court, often ordering food from his deli, so we offered him a chair.

He was a little man of middle eastern descent, neatly dressed in a white shirt buttoned to the neck, soft spoken and very correct, and he opened by saying that he had been observing our family every week since he had opened his little restaurant a few years before.

He said that he thought we had a lovely family and he admired the way we all got along so well and we reminded him of his family and his children who were all grown up and had families of their own.

Then he took out a business card and handed it to me. "If either of your kids are in need of employment, it would be my pleasure to hire them to work in my little establishment." He stood, I stood, I thanked him, we shook hands, and he went back to his restaurant.

He knew not our names, our religion, our politics or where we were from, but he saw some of the fruit that our family tree had produced and that was enough for him.

Our kids never did work for that gentleman, having found jobs closer to home to which they could ride their bicycles, but even after they went off to college, when Jean and I would go to the mall to see a movie and have our Sunday dinner, we would wave to him and he would enquire, "How are your kids?"

Fruit Of The Christian Tree

You and I, brothers and sisters, are the fruit of the Christian tree. Other people see us and, knowing that we are what my grandmother used to call "church people," they inspect to see just what kind of fruit we are and make judgments about the tree that produced us.

They look for spots and blemishes in our character, bruises and rotten places in our skin and flesh, they squeeze, sniff, press, shake, and maybe even give us a thump or two and they make judgments about Jesus and his church based upon what they observe in us.

In his book, *You Lost Me,* David Kinnaman, president of the Barna Group research organization, used data collected from more than 5000 interviews of 18 — 29-year-old young adults, along with 27 years of collected data to find out how young adults perceive the human "fruit" being produced by the tree that is the church. His findings are, to say the least, distressing:

The Top Six Reasons People Age 17-29 Give For Leaving The Church

1. **The church is defensive and overprotective.**
It kills creativity and self-expression, is hypercritical and afraid of popular culture. It demonizes the secular and denies the complexity of the real world.
2. **The church is shallow.**
Church people are more interested in the form of Christianity than the substance of it. Church is all about clichés, Bible quotes, and easy answers. Little, actual Christ-like living goes on in the church. It is boring, irrelevant, and passionless. The Bible is not taught clearly or often enough and there is no sense of awe, mystery, wonder, or power.
3. **The church is anti-science.**
It is anti-intellectual, requiring us to choose between faith and science. It is too confident that it has all the answers and tries to make complex things too simple. The church is out of step with the modern world.
4. **The church is repressive.**
Especially in the area of human sexuality. The church's desire is to control people. The church's teachings about sexuality are out of step with the times. If people make mistakes in their sexual choices and behavior, they will be harshly judged by the church.
5. **The church is exclusive.**
It is unable to embrace the open-mindedness, tolerance, and acceptance that young people esteem as an ultimate value. This is especially true when it comes to accepting gay people, ethnic minority people, people of other religious faiths, and poor people. Young people feel that they will have to choose between their faith and their friends.
6. **The church is doubtless.**
Doubts can't be freely expressed and, when doubts are expressed, they are met with arguments to persuade them that they are wrong. The church is more interested in winning arguments than winning people.

Jesus' admonition that we will be judged by the way we judge others is, it would seem, spot on. It is found in the two verses that precede today's lesson:

> Do not judge, and you will not be judged; do not condemn, and you will not be condemned. Forgive, and you will be forgiven; give, and it will be given to you. A good measure, pressed down, shaken together, running over, will be put into your lap; for the measure you give will be the measure you get back (Luke 6: 37-38).

Likewise, while we are inspecting the fruit of other trees, we must always remember that our fruit and, subsequently, our tree is being inspected as well.

Lest Ye Be Judged

On July 7, 2017, about 800 people gathered peacefully in downtown Dallas to protest the shootings of two black men who were killed by police officers in Minnesota and Louisiana.

The protest march was winding down and people were heading back to their cars when shots began to ring out of the shadows and police responded with their own gunfire. When the smoke cleared, four Dallas Police Department officers and one Dallas Area Rapid Transit officer were killed. Another nine police officers were injured along with two civilians.

The gunman, Micah Johnson, was also killed by a police department bomb.

Writing in a Facebook piece in the wake of the Dallas shootings, economist and former Labor Secretary Robert Reich, said this:

> I don't recall a period when the divisions in America have seemed so stark — black and white, Muslim and non-Muslim, foreign-born and native-born, Latino and non-Latino, gay and straight, conservative and liberal. It's a fantasy to suppose we've ever been totally and effortlessly united, but I'm not sure why we're so divided right now. Are the po-

> lice more brutal? Have economic stresses made us angrier? Can we blame the demagogues and denizens of rightwing media? Is it the internet, and easy transmission of violent images and hateful words?[5]

Trevor Noah, then the host of "The Daily Show," made very much the same observation but bookended it with humor in his commentary, as described by "The Daily Beast:"

> "You know, the hardest part of having a conversation surrounding police shootings in America, it always feels like in America, it's like if you take a stand for something, you automatically are against something else." He said he understands how someone can be a "cat person or a dog person" or like the Red Sox versus the Yankees.
>
> "But with police shootings, it shouldn't have to work that way," he continued. "For instance, if you're pro Black Lives Matter you're assumed to be anti-police, and if you're pro-police, then you surely hate black people.
>
> "When in reality, you can be pro-cop and problack, which is what we should all be!" Noah said to cheers from the crowd. "That is what we should be aiming for."[6]

Interesting, is it not, that it isn't the clergy but a former politician/economist and a comedian whom we hear speaking words no less prophetic than those of Amos and Isaiah.

What they are both pointing to, I believe, is the haste and degree to which we're willing to pass judgment and the stridency with which we insist that others, especially people in positions of power, pass judgment on those with whom we disagree and from whom we feel divided.

It takes not more than a few moments on Facebook to realize

5 https://www.facebook.com/RBReich/posts/1252505568095370
6 http://www.thedailybeast.com/articles/2016/07/08/daily-show-s-trevor-noah-on-police-shootings-you-can-be-pro-cop-and-pro-black.html

that judgment is what many have come there to deliver. Harsh criticism, hateful evaluations, and mean-spirited retorts abound. People are outraged at the slightest hint of a slight or an insult and respond with brutal invective and massive overkill.

Disrespect, indignity, scorn, shame, slander, and scurrility rule. And what is it that people feel gives them permission to behave like this, to treat others this way? Why, *judgment*, of course. They have judged other persons as insignificant and undeserving of anything but their contempt.

And, as has always been the case, the most extreme persons feel empowered to act on their judgment, most often with unguarded words, but in other, more physical ways as well. Bad cops abuse their authority, aggrieved snipers murder innocent peace officers, world leaders engaging in "regime change," candidates for office exchange insults rather than ideas, and religious extremists set off bombs.

And few are those who examine the fruit of these actions born of judgment. Few are those who count the bodies, or even take the time to know the names of those who died. Our water cooler discussions tend toward figuring out upon which side of judgment we should stand rather than how we can help the injured and the aggrieved.

God, the Lord of history, and the Creator of all things is, for people of faith, the only one qualified to be the moral judge of human beings and God's judgment always falls on the side of forgiveness, grace, and love. When we take that responsibility upon ourselves, another picture tends to emerge, the fruit we produce may look ripe and beautiful at first, but a closer inspection will often show it to be full of worms and rot.

If we are to be the licensed fruit inspectors that Jesus calls us to be, we would do well to begin by shining the light of grace on our own lives and taking a long look at our own actions and the actions of our institutions and the fruit they produce.

Proper 4

Luke 7: 1-10

Surprised By The Kingdom

> A centurion there had a slave whom he valued highly, and who was ill and close to death. When he heard about Jesus, he sent some Jewish elders to him, asking him to come and heal his slave.
>
> Luke 7:2b-3

What Was A Centurion?

To understand the full impact of this passage, we have to start with a little Roman history, specifically, Roman army history.

The first records we have that tell us anything about how the Roman army was organized, date back to about 800 BCE, but they aren't very helpful for understanding things in the first century CE, Jesus' time, as the army evolved and changed over the years. During the first century, what we would call New Testament times, the Roman army was, with some notable exceptions, organized pretty much like this:

> At the time of Jesus, the Roman army consisted of about thirty legions.
>
> A legion had anywhere from 3,000 to 5,000 soldiers and was commanded by a legate (today = general).
>
> A legion was divided into centuries, each containing 100-150 soldiers commanded by a centurion.
>
> Centuries were grouped into cohorts, each containing 5-10 centuries. Each cohort was commanded by a Tribune (colonel or captain) or a Primus (today = lieutenant), the senior most centurion.

Centurions were always promoted from within the ranks as a reward for their courage, fidelity to the legion, and proven leadership skills in battle. Often caricatured for their muscled calves and hobnailed boots, centurions held the roughly equivalent rank of a sergeant-major in today's army.

By Jesus' time, senior centurions, besides serving in the legions, were also appointed to administrative positions in the occupied territories, positions which usually had to do with enforcing Roman law, keeping the peace, settling disputes, and collecting taxes. These centurions were wildly unpopular in the territories and, in Palestine, they were no doubt often the targets of the Jewish Zealots and Sicarii assassins. For this reason, among others, centurions in administrative or law enforcement positions were usually given a smaller century of thirty to fifty soldiers to assist them in their work.

There were six centurions mentioned in the New Testament, all of them in a positive light.

1. The first centurion at the Antonia Fortress (Acts 22) assisted in rescuing Paul from an angry mob and then saved him from being flogged.
2. The second centurion at the Antonia Fortress (Acts 23) saved Paul from an assassination attempt by the Sadducees.
3. Julius was described as a centurion of the prestigious Augustin Cohort and it was he who saved Paul from being killed by mutinous seamen when their ship ran aground (Acts 27).
4. Cornelius, a centurion at Caesarea, was one of the first Gentile converts to Christianity (Acts 10).
5. The unnamed centurion at Calvary confessed Jesus as a "righteous man" in Luke 15 and as "the Son of God" in Matthew 27 and Mark 15.
6. Finally, we come to the subject of today's story, the man known, simply, as "the centurion at Capernaum."

The Centurion At Capernaum

The story of the centurion at Capernaum finds its source in what biblical scholars call "Q."

Q is an anonymous source that was known to Matthew and Luke but was not known to Mark, as none of the Q stories appeared in Mark. When they appeared in Matthew and Luke they were often identical, word-for-word in some parts but with significant differences in others.

I'll note the similarities and differences as we walk through Luke's version of the story:

> In Matthew's gospel, Jesus concluded the Sermon on the Mount, came down the mountain and healed a leper, then proceeded to Capernaum. Luke began the story with the conclusion of the Sermon on the Plain in chapter 6 and Jesus arriving in Capernaum, immediately in the opening lines of chapter 7.
>
> Luke illustrated the lessons of the Sermon on the Plain with three stories that exemplify the radical and inclusive nature of life in the kingdom. In the three stories, we will see Jesus defy cultural and religious taboos by the way he treats a gentile, Roman soldier, a widow and her deceased son, and a woman of ill repute in the community.

In the first of the three stories, the one under consideration today, Jesus arrived in Capernaum, a small fishing village of about 200 households on the north shore of the Sea of Galilee. It appeared from the gospel witness that Jesus used Capernaum as the hub for his ministry, as he left from and returned to there several times. Peter's home was there and there are more than a few stories of Jesus teaching and healing people there. Some scholars cite a passage in Mark's gospel (2:1) that implies that Jesus may have owned a home there. Whether that was or was not the case, he was there often and would have been a familiar presence in such a small village.

In Matthew's version of the story, a centurion came to Jesus and begged for his help. In Luke's version, the centurion never actually appeared but is referred to by his friends who came on his behalf.

Luke laid the groundwork in the introduction of the story: There was a centurion in the town who had a slave who was ill and close to death. (Matthew told us that it was not a slave but a servant who was paralyzed and dying.)

The centurion was probably a senior member of his rank serving an administrative post in Capernaum and the small towns in the surrounding area: Magdala, Gennesaret, Korazin and, probably, Bethsaida. As we have noted, he would have had a garrison of 30-50 soldiers under his command and it would have been his responsibility to enforce Roman law, keep the peace, settle disputes, and collect taxes.

The servant (or slave) who was dying was probably what was called a batman, a soldier assigned to be the assistant to and orderly for an officer. In this case the centurion and his batman had become close, perhaps even friends, and the centurion was worried that his trusted and beloved assistant might die.

In Matthew's gospel, the centurion, hearing that Jesus was in town and probably knowing of Jesus' reputation, came to Jesus, himself, and said, "My servant is lying at home paralyzed, in terrible distress." Jesus responded, immediately, "I will come and cure him."

Luke told the story differently, dragging it out some. In Luke's version, the centurion never actually showed up in the story. He was a background figure that, worried about his servant but knowing that Jesus was a Jew, went to the Jewish leaders in the community, what we would think of as the elders of the church, and asked them to speak to Jesus on his behalf and (wonder of wonders) they did.

Now, let's pause here, for just a moment to consider the full import of what is happening. Remember, the Romans were an occupying army. The mass of the army may have gone back home to Rome or off to fight on other frontiers, but Roman appointed governors and centurions with soldiers under their command, living symbols of Roman oppression, had been left behind to enforce Rome's will.

We may not always like the way our police, our politicians, or our tax collectors behave but remember, those police are enforcing *our* laws, those politicians were put in place by *our* votes, and the IRS is collecting *our* taxes to fund *our* government.

Not so in Roman occupied Palestine.

Those Romans were there to enforce Roman law and they had been put there by Caesar, not by the people, and the taxes they were collecting were Roman taxes levied to make Rome rich. So, make no mistake, the Romans were, with a few notable exceptions, roundly hated by the Palestinian Jews of that time. And one of those notable exceptions is this group of Jewish leaders who have come to Jesus.

Having a background in theater, as I do, I love to think of these stories as scenes and I can imagine this one unfolding before us, the audience, with no small amount of humor written into the lines.

The Jewish leaders come running up to Jesus and stop him. "Jesus, there is an important and powerful man in the community and his servant, whom he loves, is very sick and may, in fact, be dying. Will you please come and see if maybe you can heal this man's servant?"

Jesus: Who is this man? Maybe I know him.

Leader 1: Oh, no, no. You wouldn't know him. No.

Jesus: Well, what makes him so powerful and why didn't he come and ask me himself?

Leader 2: Well, you see, he, uh...

Jesus: What does he do? How does he make a living?

Leader 3: Oh, you know, he uh, he uh...

Jesus: What are you trying to hide from me? Who is this guy?

Leader 1: (as he covers his mouth to cough) He's a *Rmmn Cntrn.*

Jesus: A what?

Leader: A centurion, okay? He's a Roman Centurion!

Leader 2: But he's a really nice guy.

Leader 3: He treats us well.

Leader 1: And he paid to build our synagogue.

Leader 2: And sometimes he comes by and asks questions because he wants to learn about our faith.

Leader 3: And sometimes he comes on the Sabbath and sits in the gentile section and worships with us.

Leader 1: Come on, Jesus. Please. He really is a stand-up guy and he needs your help.

Jesus: Well, okay, why didn't you say so? Let's go.

(They start walking, as a group, toward the centurion's house when another group of Jews meets them.)

Leader A: Ah, Jesus, just the man we were looking for. We need to talk.

Jesus: Yeah, in a minute, I'm on my way to the centurion's house to…

Leader B: That's what we need to talk about.

Leader C: See, the centurion sent us, and he says that he knows that you're an observant Jew and entering a gentile house would make you ritually unclean and unable to enter the temple. He says that, being a vile, unclean gentile, he is not worthy for you to enter his home.

Leader A: He asks that you heal his servant from here.

Leader B: He says that he's a man of power and authority...

Leader C: He says, "Jump," and his soldiers say, *"how high?"*

Leader A: He says, "Fish," and people say, *"how deep?*

Leader B: He says, "Run," and people say, *"how fast?"*

Leader C: He says,...

Leader A: He gets the picture, okay? At any rate, Jesus, he says he knows a man of authority and power when he sees one and you are one. He says that you can order the sickness to leave his servant from here and it will obey you. Is that true? Can you do that?

Jesus: *(Looking around.)* Can I? Can I? He's a gentile, a Roman soldier and he's got more faith than you. In fact, I've not seen anyone with this kind of faith in all of Israel. (To his disciples) No offense.

Peter: None taken.

(The second group of Jews dash off to the centurion's house.)

Jesus: What is it with us Jews? Why do we always just assume that God's going to approve of us no matter what we do or how little faith we show? I'm telling you, when the judgment comes, we're going to be shocked to see people of every creed and color entering the kingdom ahead of us. I keep saying it and you refuse to listen: The first will be last...

Disciples: *(In unison)* and the last will be first.

(The leaders look at each other and shrug. They have no idea what Jesus is talking about.) (The group who went to the centurion's house return, running and panting.)

Leader A: He did it. The servant, what's his name...

Leader B: Milenius.

Leader A: Yeah, the servant, Milenius. He's cured.

Leader C: Sitting up on the side of his bed, sipping some chicken soup and talking.

Leader A: He's weak, but they say he'll be fine.

Leader B: *(to A and C)* I thought his color looked good, didn't you?

Leader A and C: Very good, yes...totally in the pink...very natural. *(and so on)*

(All Jewish leaders turn and walk away.) I've never seen anything like that...Doesn't that just beat all?... Amazing! *(and more)*

Even A Roman

The kingdom is often found where we least expect to find it. Certainly, the early readers of Luke's gospel didn't expect to find it in a Roman centurion. He was a nice guy, certainly. He was good to the Jews, even kind and generous. He was decent and fair.

Too bad he was going to hell when he died.

We hear that, don't we? We hear it from well-meaning Christians. It doesn't matter how good you are, how well you treat other people, how perfectly you exemplify the golden rule, if you don't — and here's the key, the secret formula that will get you into heaven — if you don't "accept and make a public confession of Jesus Christ as your personal Lord and Savior," you're going to hell to suffer eternal pain and torment after you die.

But this story puts the lie to that kind of nonsense, does it not? Jesus heals the centurion's servant. No questions asked. No qualifications required. The centurion may or may not be a believer. He may be nothing more than a nice guy. And, certainly, there is no indication that the sick servant is a believer.

We have no evidence that either servant or master converted and became faithful Jews or Christians after this story.

All we have is Jesus recognizing good in another person, a person that would otherwise have been despised, and rewarding that good with healing.

Betty was a member of my church and had spent her entire life content to be a farmer's wife, a mom, a grandma, and an active and faithful member of her church.

In her early eighties, she was a vibrant and busy person, and one day, while working in her garden, she fell over with a heart attack. One of the hired men saw her fall and rushed to her assistance. He called 9-1-1 and within a few minutes, the volunteer fire department had whisked her off to the hospital where, the next day, she underwent coronary bypass surgery.

Two days later, I was sitting at her bedside with several members of her family and she was chattering away about this and that, when her nurse a young man in his early thirties, named Joseph, came in, waved his arms around and announced that "there are altogether too many people in this room, having too much fun. It's time for Ms. Betty's morning ablutions. Now, everyone go down to the cafeteria, have a donut and a coffee and let Joseph do his job."

As we filed out of her room, he reminded us that, "She'll be tired after that so only one person at a time in the room. Pastor, you go first. You all can come back this afternoon if you want. Now shoo!"

About forty minutes later I was back in Betty's room. She was freshly bathed, perfumed, her hair combed, and her makeup on and she was sitting up in bed, tired but content, holding a teddy bear against her chest. She allowed that a teddy bear was given to all heart surgery patients to squeeze when they did their breathing exercises. I noted that she looked very good, considering that she had just had open heart surgery less than 48 hours before.

"Thanks to Joseph," she said. "I just love him." Then, almost conspiratorially, "He's gay as the Fourth of July, you know."

I allowed that I did, in fact, know. I'd been on this floor many times and Joseph and I knew each other.

"Well, Dean, that man has taken wonderful care of me. He's just so caring and so loving." she sighed. "Well, I've decided that I'm going to have to rethink everything I believed about homosexuality. I just can't believe that God doesn't love Joseph as much as I do." She paused and then added. "And as much as Joseph loves his patients."

The kingdom of God can sneak up on you, you know? It can show up where and when you least expect it.

It showed up in a small fishing village called Capernaum, on the shore of the Sea of Galilee, two thousand years ago, in the person of a Roman centurion.

Or, today, it may show up in a room on the cardiac surgery unit of a large metropolitan hospital, in the person of a gay nurse.

You just never know.

So maybe we'd better keep our eyes and our minds open, right? Amen.

Proper 5

Luke 7: 11-17

Hopeless Isn't Hopeless Anymore

> When the Lord saw her, he had compassion for her and said to her, "Do not weep."
> Luke 13

The town of Nain still exists and lies about 32 miles southwest of Capernaum, where the previous story took place. A well-paved road connects the two towns and you can drive from one to the other in about 45 minutes. In the time of this story, it would have been about a two-day walk.

Today, Nain is a small village of about twenty houses but in Jesus' time, it was probably a town of some serious size and importance. Tombs located in the hillside above the present town indicate a size of probably somewhere in the neighborhood of 1,000 homes. Olives and grapes were the primary cash crop of the area along with something called *simsum,* the nature of which we do not know, though some historians speculate that it may have been an aromatic plant used in the making of incense.

The name, Nain, means "lovely" and probably was given to the town because it sat on the side of a prominent hill known as "Little Hermon" and offered a panoramic view of the olive and fig groves and vineyards below as well as the Plain of Esdraelon and, on a clear day, the town of Nazareth, some miles away.

It is in this town that Jesus and his disciples arrive shortly after the healing of the centurion's servant. No doubt, they were on an emotional high after a victory such as that. We can imagine them walking with a bounce in their step, joking and laughing with each other as they went.

"A centurion! Can you imagine?" or "Did you see the looks on their faces when those guys came back and said that the servant was healed?" or "Boy, I've never known a centurion like that." Or "Wish we could have met him."

But their good-natured banter was brought up short as they approach the village.

Here, before them, came one of the most solemn and serious spectacles a human being could encounter: a funeral procession. And not just any funeral procession, this was an ancient, Middle Eastern, Hebrew funeral procession.

As is the custom, today, in the Middle East, the dead were, in Jesus' time, buried on the day they died. Outside of Egypt, there was no method for embalming, so the fear of infection or defilement dictated that the bodies be buried quickly.

Again, outside of Egypt, coffins were, generally, not used. The body of the deceased would be prepared for burial by the family, washed and dressed in their best garb or with the wealthy, clothing purchased especially for the funeral. If the family was poor, the body was simply wrapped in cloths or a simple, long, shirt-like garment. While the body was being prepared, members of the family would go to the tomb, usually a cave, natural or hand-carved in the side of a hill and prepare the ledge or platform where the body would be placed. The tombs were usually reused so the bones of previous burials would be removed from the ledge and placed in a *reliquary,* a box made for that purpose and stacked with other such boxes at the back of the tomb. If the family could not afford to have a reliquary built, the bones were usually just piled near the back of the tomb with others.

The body was then placed on a "bier," a flat litter or plank that was decorated by the family, and carried to the tomb. The procession would be made up of family and friends of the deceased and, if the family could afford it, professional mourners who were paid to create a chorus of wailing to announce to one and all the depth of the family's grief.

The body was then placed in the tomb and, depending on local or religious custom, the time of mourning, which could last anywhere from a day to a month, would commence.

The particular funeral procession which Jesus and the disciples stumbled upon was emerging from the gate of the town as they approached. (Archeologists have found no trace of a wall around the town of Nain, so the "gate" mentioned was probably the place where the main road entered and went through the town.)

Jesus looked at the procession and could tell by the order in which people were walking and how they were arranged that the lone woman walking there was a widow and the man being buried was her only son, the last member of her family. This funeral was a painful one in several respects.

The Grief And Pain Of Loss

First, there is the pain and grief that accompanies the loss of one we love.

I have presided at more funerals than I can count, and I've never been at one that didn't involve pain. Oh, we can say those things that we sometimes say, that "she lived a long, full life," or "he was ready to go," or "it's a blessing, really." All of those may be true.

I have buried people who were ready to die, to move on to the next stage of existence, whatever it was. I have buried people who were in terrible and agonizing pain right up to the point where the analgesics and narcotics they were being given played a significant role in their passing. I have buried people whose families breathed an often, secret sigh of relief that they were finally released from the agony and responsibility of watching and caring for a mother or father who was not really living so much as they were lingering.

And I remember one particular funeral that I was asked to conduct for a family who had no church home. The man who had died was, the funeral director assured me, hateful and abusive to his family; a mean drunk of whom his wife and two daughters lived in constant fear. The deceased, a relatively young man in his mid-fifties, had gotten drunk and driven his car off the road and into a tree, killing himself, much to the relief of his family. The funeral, I was told, should be kept relatively short, straightforward, and unsentimental.

The funeral director accompanied me into the chapel and there were the three women, wife and daughters, bawling their eyes out, wailing and crying, sobbing and all but throwing themselves on the casket.

I looked at him and he looked at me and we both shrugged. Apparently, there was in them a splinter of grief for, if nothing else, the man he might have been and never was and was now lost before he could become.

Like I said, I've never presided at a funeral in which there wasn't at least a little and, in most, a lot of pain. That's how loss is.

And the pain reaches its zenith when the funeral is one where parents are burying their child.

We have no trouble imagining and accepting that this type of grief is particularly painful. I, personally, have come to realize that there is, in all of life, no grief, no pain, no misery as deep and profound as that of a parent who loses a child. We are, simply, not built for that.

Life prepares us for loss. As we grow and mature through childhood, youth, young adulthood, middle age, and, finally, old age, we experience different kinds of losses as we go and they are usually just part of what it means to be a growing, changing human being.

As a child, we enjoy playing on the playground and look forward to going to the park where all the playground equipment stands. Then, one spring, we show up at the park only to discover that we no longer fit on the swings or the slide. The merry-go-round won't accommodate our longer legs, and our feet touch the ground no matter how high we climb on the monkey bars. Life has taken from us the playground and we experience some grief that accompanies that loss as we watch our younger siblings still enjoying the things we've outgrown.

As we get older, life continues to teach us how to handle loss by giving us losses from time to time. Our parent gets transferred and we have to move away from our friends. Our pet grows old and dies. Our boyfriend breaks up with us, our voice changes and we are no longer the star of the children's choir, grandma passes away. One by one, life teaches us about loss and we learn to experience grief and, eventually, move past it and onto the rest of our lives.

But life does not teach us how to lose a child. Nothing that life can throw at us can prepare us for that searing, burning, pain that leaves us with a hollow place in our soul that will never be filled again. We'll learn to live with it and even, from time to time, to suppress it. But it never goes away completely.

And, I have found, that is true whether the child is two, twenty, or seventy years of age. The pain which the parent feels is just as profound whether they are twenty, fifty, or hundred years old.

When we survive such horrible pain and grief, and we usually, miraculously, do, in large part, because we have friends and family to guide us through it. We are not left alone. Unlike the widow at Nain. She was left totally alone.

Abandonment

Before Social Security was enacted in 1935, the poorest people in America were the elderly. Most, when they became too old to work, were destitute. They had to move in with family and, if there was no family to take care of them, they had to rely on the kindness of charities and strangers, of which there were few, indeed.

In 1929, 56% of people over 65 and 65% of people over seventy were totally dependent upon others for their essential needs — food, shelter, medicine, clothing, etc. More than half lived with relatives or friends. 8 – 10% of all people over 65 lived in charity communities, poorhouses, mental hospitals, or "homes for the aged."[7]

Today, 97% of people over sixty receive Social Security benefits. For about 45% of those recipients, Social Security represents 90% or more of their income. On average, that's about $435 per month. (Social Security Administration [SSA], 2016)

So, even with Social Security, most of our elderly people need

7 https://www.seniorliving.orgf/history/1900-1929/

assistance from either a pension or the good will of their friends, families, or charities. Churches have usually been in the forefront of those providing help for the indigent elderly.

Now, if that's how things are, today, imagine how they must have been for that poor widow in the town of Nain. As she walked, alone behind the funeral bier of her only son, it was not just grief that bent her over and weighed upon her shoulders, it was also despair.

She was now, utterly alone. She was at the mercy of whatever charitable inclinations might dwell within her neighbors and, if the words of the prophets are any clue, those charitable inclinations were few and far between. Listen to what the prophets said of this state of affairs:

> Isaiah reminds the people of the charity they have forgotten how to give "...learn to do good; seek justice, rescue the oppressed, defend the orphan, plead for the widow" (Isaiah 1:17).
>
> Ezekiel condemns the behavior of the aristocracy of Israel: "Father and mother are treated with contempt in you; the alien residing within you suffers extortion; the orphan and the widow are wronged in you" (Ezehiel 22: 7).
>
> Malachi puts those who are not charitable to widows and orphans in the same category as sorcerers, adulterers, liars, and slave drivers: "Then I will draw near to you for judgment; I will be swift to bear witness against the sorcerers, against the adulterers, against those who swear falsely, against those who oppress the hired workers in their wages, the widow and the orphan, against those who thrust aside the alien..." (Malachi 3:5).

Widows, because they were alone and desperate, were vulnerable. They were easy to cheat and extort and often driven by unscrupulous landlords, money lenders, and employers, into beggary or prostitution.

Jesus sees this poor woman, notes her situation, and feels "compassion" for her.

Sympathy Vs. Empathy

We hear a great deal these days about empathy. It has, to a large degree, replaced sympathy as a value in our culture. Empathy is often considered a deeper, more profound, more valuable asset in relating to others. Sympathy is often scoffed at as shallow and sentimental but of little authentic value in human relationships.

A person who is incapable of feeling empathy is usually described as a sociopath.

A person who does not feel sympathy for others is often admired for being wisely prudent and practical.

The correct definitions of the words, however, tend to run toward something like this:

> Empathy is what you have when you understand another person's feelings because you have had a similar experience to the one that person is having but you do not necessarily share that person's feelings. We have all been disappointed, for instance, so we understand the feelings of someone else who is disappointed even when we are not, necessarily, disappointed ourselves. "I know and understand your disappointment at not getting to go to the ball game. I however, am not a baseball fan, so I'm not, personally, disappointed."
>
> Sympathy is when we understand the feelings of another and actually share those feelings. "I know and understand your disappointment at not getting to go to the ball game and I am also disappointed because I wanted to go to the ball game, too."

Empathy is often referred to as "the moral imagination." Sympathy does not require imagination. It is a shared experience.

Empathy leads to understanding but it does not necessarily lead to compassion. Sympathy almost always leads to compassion because, etymologically, the words have the same meaning: to suffer together, or to share suffering with another.

When Jesus looked upon the widow, he did not simply understand how she felt, he actually felt it with her. Her sorrow was his sorrow. Her grief was his grief. Her despair was his despair.

But Jesus went two steps beyond understanding her feelings and one step beyond sharing them. He actually acted to alleviate her suffering and despair. His sympathy led him to act sympathetically.

First, he said something outrageous: "Do not weep."

What must her friends from the town have thought upon hearing him say this? Was he nuts? Why shouldn't she weep? Her only son had died. Or maybe he was just insensitive and unsympathetic.

How often do we set the standard for sympathy and compassion and condemn those who don't meet it by living up to our expectations? A truly sympathetic person, we say, would hug her or stroke her hand. How insensitive of him to say, "do not weep." Of course, she can weep.

But what if she doesn't weep? What would we think of her then? What if she is the one who doesn't meet our expectations for a grieving mother?

In his thought-provoking book, *Talking to Strangers,* author Malcom Gladwell told the story of Amanda Marie Knox, an American woman who spent almost four years in an Italian prison following her conviction for the 2007 murder of Meredith Kercher, a fellow exchange student who shared her apartment.

In 2015, Knox was definitively acquitted by the Italian Supreme Court of Cassation. The court found that there was virtually no evidence against her and she was convicted on the grounds that she didn't meet the expectations of the police and prosecutors for a person who was grieving over the murder of her roommate.

So, Jesus broke a social taboo by not meeting peoples' expectations of a sympathetic person.

Then he broke a religious taboo by touching the funeral

bier, the stretcher-like thing that the body was being carried on. Observant Jews did not touch corpses or things corpses touched. If they did so, they would have to undergo ritual baths and other cleansing rites before they could enter the temple in Jerusalem. But Jesus ignored this taboo and touched the funeral bier.

"Young man," he said, "I say to you, rise."

The son did, in fact, rise, and everyone backed away and proclaimed that Jesus was, indeed, one powerful prophet.

Well, I should say. He had raised the dead. But, more importantly, he had changed the parameters that had, heretofore, separated that which was hopeful from that which was hopeless.

Death, you see, has always been considered pretty much hopeless.

But not anymore.

From now on, hope is a viable option, even in the face of that which we always thought was hopeless. Hope actually comes walking out of the shadows and into the sunlight and everyone sees it and is amazed.

Thanks to Jesus, hopeless isn't hopeless anymore.

Brothers and sisters, how is that one proven fact going to change your life this week? This month? This year? How can we be and live as people of hope in a hopeless world?

For that is what Jesus is asking us to do. Amen.

Proper 6

Luke 7:36 – 8:3

I, Pharisee

> Now when the Pharisee who had invited him saw it, he said to himself, "If this man were a prophet, he would have known who and what kind of woman this is who is touching him — that she is a sinner."
>
> Luke 7:39

The summer between my sophomore and junior year in high school, my father got a huge offer from another company that he accepted. With only a few weeks' notice, we sold our house, packed up all our belongings, and left the city where I had lived the first sixteen years of my life, the city where all my friends lived, where I liked the people and was liked in return, and moved to another city where I knew no one.

We arrived in August, just in time to join the football team and take part in two-a-day practices. Classes started the day after Labor Day and my brother (a freshman) and I wandered through the doors of that place — total strangers to all but a few that we encountered.

We met some people through football, band, and choir. And we met a few others via the church youth group. We gradually started eating lunch with someone besides each other and learning our way around the hallways and the various nuanced byways of high school culture as it existed in that school in 1967.

One of the things I learned was that the homecoming dance, which took place in October, was a Sadie Hawkins dance, one where, by custom, the girls invited the boys to be their dates.

Being a member of the student body for less than four weeks, I didn't know many girls and didn't expect to be invited to the dance. To be honest, it was kind of a relief. I didn't need the extra stress that a homecoming dance at a new school would have meant.

But I enjoyed that sense of relief too soon.

One day, as I was coming out of the cafeteria, on my way to chemistry class, I was approached by a tall, lanky girl I had seen in a couple of my classes. She was nearly as tall as my 6'3", probably just a hair over 6'0". She was attractive in an edgy way — a little too much makeup, skirt a little too short, and hair a little too big. But I could see a reasonably attractive girl under all the overdone stuff. She was flanked on either side by two of her girlfriends — shorter, rounder versions of herself.

She stopped in front of me. I stopped. She introduced herself in case I didn't know who she was and I assured her that I did though I really only knew her first name. Her last name was new to me.

She took a deep breath and then blurted out, "Dean, would you like to go to homecoming with me?" My first response to the word "homecoming" was that she was talking about the game and didn't realize that I was on the football team and would be playing. Then my brain caught up and I realized that she was talking about the dance, the Sadie Hawkins dance and she was inviting me to be her date.

"Uh, sure," I said.

She smiled a huge grin and I noticed a little lipstick on her front teeth. "Great," she said. "Okay. We'll talk later, okay?"

"Okay," I said.

"Okay, great," she said. She turned and walked away with her wingmen, all of them giggling.

By Sunday night, the news of my date had run its course through the Youth Fellowship and I was immediately surrounded by my new friends. The girls were appalled that I was intending to go to the homecoming dance with "that girl." The guys greeted me with sly winks and lecherous nods.

Didn't I know that she had a "reputation?" They used some words and language that are not appropriate, here, but indicated that she was a person of loose morals. She was, they said, notoriously "fast." And then there were all the rumors about venereal diseases, abortions, and other unacceptable behaviors, some felonious in nature.

You have to break it off, the girls said. *You have to tell us what happens,* the boys said. *You're new here,* they all said. *You don't want people to get the wrong ideas about you. You're known by the company you keep.*

I wish I could tell you that I ignored their alarmist warnings, their mean rumors, and their salacious grins and giggles. I wish I could tell you that I opted for kindness and acceptance and grace, instead. I wish I could tell you that.

But I was a 16-year-old teenager, unsure of myself in a new community, a new school, and a new church. I was anxious about my own reputation, how others would see me, what they would think of me. So, on Monday I caught up to the girl who would have me as her date to homecoming. And I lied.

Conjuring up all the fake consternation I could muster, I told her that I had a theretofore unknown out of town family obligation and would not be able to attend the homecoming dance with her. Before I even finished the sentence, I saw the disappointment and hurt in her eyes and I wanted to take it back. She knew it was a lie. She knew that I was a coward who only pretended to be a nice guy, a kind and accepting guy who gave people a chance.

She was classy enough not to confront me and call me out. She just said, "Oh, okay." And she turned and walked away. A few weeks later she was gone from the school to no one knew where and I never got the chance to apologize or make it up to her. There were rumors, of course, but those rumors I ignored. It was the least I could do.

That was over fifty years ago and I am still haunted by the look of pain and disappointment in her eyes. In my heart I wanted to be like Jesus but, when the occasion arose, I was like the Pharisee.

Luke completed the sermon on the plain in chapter 6 of his gospel and, in chapter 7, he launched into a series of three stories which demonstrated the lessons of grace, love, kindness, and inclusion that he had taught in the sermon.

In 7:1-10, Jesus encountered a Roman centurion who would have normally been hated by the Jews but was, in fact, loved by them because of how he treated them. Jesus accepted their acceptance of him and said that the soldier has demonstrated a greater faith than those Pharisees who only showed up to judge and reject.

In 7:11-17, Jesus was overcome with compassion and sympathy for a widow and allowed that such responses to human suffering were more important than traditional, cultural taboos. He then violated the taboo by touching the funeral bier and raising the widow's deceased son back to life.

In 7:18-35, Jesus was interrupted by some followers of John the Baptist who asked if he is the Messiah. Jesus answered not with a theological treatise but with a simple observation, a play on the tree/fruit metaphor: What does scripture say the Messiah will do and what do you see me doing?

Then, in 7:35-8:3, Luke concluded this section with the story of a "sinful" woman who was accepted with kindness by Jesus and reminding his readers of the important role of women in the early church. But, before we get more deeply into the text, it might be helpful to examine, as context, the role of women in general in the first century.

Women In The Early Church[8]

The synoptic gospels (Matthew, Mark, and Luke) all report that women played a significant role in the life and ministry of Jesus. They were present throughout the gospels, at his execution long after the men fled away, and they were the first witnesses to his resurrection, insisting on its veracity even when the men refused to believe them (Luke 24: 11).

Biblical and extra-biblical sources list women among the most active and important leaders of the early churches in the cities of the Roman Empire — Priscilla, Chloe, Lydia, Apphia, Nympha,

8 For the information in this section, I am indebted to the Christian History Institute and their article "The Neglected History of Women in the Early Church," adapted from the article "Women in the Early Church," in Christian History magazine. https://christianhistoryinstitute.org/magazine/article/women-in-the-early-church/

the mother of John, Mark, and possibly the "elect lady" of John's second epistle.

In the second century, Clement of Alexandria wrote that the apostles were accompanied on their missionary journeys by women who were not marriage partners, but colleagues, "that they might be their fellow ministers in dealing with housewives. It was through them that the Lord's teaching penetrated also the women's quarters without any scandal being aroused. We also know the directions about women deacons which were given by the noble Paul in his letter to Timothy."

A woman named Junia was mentioned by Paul in Romans 16 as "of note among the apostles," and considered by many to be an apostle, herself.

Paul also mentioned Phoebe in Romans 16, "a deacon of the church at Cenchreae." He called her an overseer and admonished the Roman church to welcome and assist her, "For she has been appointed, actually by my own action, an officer presiding over many."

The four daughters of Philip appeared in Acts 21:9 as prophetesses. The historian, Eusebius, viewed these daughters in the same category as ordained leaders of the church.

Bishop Cyprian of Carthage, in his *Testimonia* that described a Christianity full of women such that "Christian maidens were very numerous" so that it was difficult to find Christian husbands for all of them.

Why so many women? Historians put forward several possible reasons:

Early pagans favored male offspring over female. "Exposure," was a not uncommon practice of abandoning unwanted female infants to the elements and allowing them to die. Christians repudiated this practice, so they had more living females.

Also, in the upper echelons of society, women often converted to Christianity while their male relatives remained pagans, out of fear that they might lose their senatorial status. This contributed to a large number of upper-class women in the church.

These wealthy, educated Christian women seized upon the

study of the Bible and of Hebrew and Greek. So many Roman women studied with Jerome in the late 300s that he thought nothing of referring some church elders to Marcella for the resolution of a problem of biblical interpretation. By the early 400s, Augustine declared that "any old Christian woman" was better educated in spiritual matters than many philosophers.

Christian women also became leaders in social service. Fabiola founded the first Christian hospital in Europe. Letters and diaries remind us that wealthy, Christian women encountered severe opposition from their families for spending their wealth so generously in helping the poor. Such selfless ministry became a trademark of Christian women. In a letter to his wife, Tertullian gave us a glimpse into some of the ministries of church women in his time. He charged her, in case of his own death, to not marry a pagan because a pagan husband would never allow his wife to do the things a Christian husband would allow.

"Who would be willing to let his wife go through one street after another to other men's houses, and indeed to the poorer cottages, in order to visit the brethren? Who would like to see her being taken from his side by some duty of attending a nocturnal gathering? At Easter time who would quietly tolerate her absence all the night? Who would unsuspiciously let her go to the Lord's Supper, that feast upon which they heaped such calumnies? Who would let her creep into jail to kiss the martyr's chains or bring water for the saints' feet?"

The church fathers of the second century also mentioned women as stalwarts in the faith. Twice Ignatius sent greetings to Alce, whom he called especially dear to him. He also greeted Tavia and her household; perhaps she was another house-church leader.

It is into that historic milieu that we now step as we consider Luke's account of Jesus, the Pharisee, and the sinful woman.

Jesus, The Pharisee, And The Woman

The story opened with Jesus being invited to dinner at the home of a pharisee named Simon. Nothing shocking or scandalous, there. We tend to lump all Pharisees into one, big hypocritical group but remember, Nicodemus and Paul were both Pharisees. As with all groups of people, there are good ones and not so good ones.

Jesus, Simon, and other guests were reclining at the table and the meal was going well when a woman of the city, a sinner, we are told, entered the house with an alabaster vial of ointment, found Jesus, whom she knew was in attendance, and went to him with the intention of washing his feet with the scented oil in the vial. She was overcome with emotion and, before she could open the vial, she began to weep and her tears fell upon his feet. She quickly dried them with her hair, kissed them, and applied the oil.

The woman was described as a sinner in the present sense. The sin of which she was guilty was an ongoing and perpetual one. The text did not say "a woman who once was or used to be a sinner," it said, "A woman in the city was a sinner." Most assume, and not without reason, that her sin was a sexual one. Perhaps she was carrying on an ongoing affair. Or perhaps she was a serial adulteress. Or maybe she was a prostitute. We do not know.

What we do know is that she was repentant. She was sorry, horribly, horribly sorry.

The Pharisee and his friends were not moved by her contrition. They are more interested in the fact that Jesus allowed her to touch him. If he was really a prophet, they thought, he would know what kind of woman she was and would not allow her to touch him. He would, in fact, had nothing to do with her. Clearly, he was not a true prophet.

Jesus intuits what they were thinking and, rather than defending himself, he defended the woman with a parable.

A money lender had two people who owe him money, one a little and one a lot, and neither of them could pay. He went to each and canceled their debt. Which one do you suppose would be more grateful? Which one would love the forgiving moneylender more?

Simon answered, correctly, that the one who was forgiven

more would love more in return.

In Jesus' further retort to Simon we discover that, for some reason, the Pharisee had violated one of the sacrosanct, perhaps the most sacred laws of ancient Jewry, the law of hospitality.

For some reason, either by inattention or absent mindedness, the Pharisee, an expert in the law, did not provide water for Jesus to wash his feet when he entered the house. Neither did he greet him with a kiss on the cheek, a customary greeting of any host to a guest. And, finally, Simon did not provide Jesus with a cooling and refreshing oil to cleanse his hands and face and head. Simon has, through neglect, violated one of the foundational customs and laws of first-century Judaism.

But the woman's sins were even greater. That's why she had shown Jesus such affection and love. She had been forgiven much, so her appreciation was great. Simon, on the other hand, had violated the rule of hospitality, a law which he obviously did not take very seriously. So, when he was forgiven for his moral lapse, he was not so very grateful.

Jesus then turned to the woman and announced not what he was doing but what God had already done: "Your sins are forgiven." And, as the dinner guests asked each other, "Who does he think he is, forgiving sins and whatnot?" He told the woman that her faith had saved her and she should go in peace.

Fred Craddock, in his commentary on Luke, (*Interpretation: A Bible-Commentary for Teaching and Preaching)* asked the rhetorical question of where this woman was supposed to find peace, now that her life had been transformed by grace?

"The price of the woman's way of life in the city had been removal from the very institutions that carried the resources to restore her. The one place where she was welcome is the street, among people like herself. What she needed was a community of forgiven and forgiving sinners. The story screamed the need for a church, not just any church but one that said, "You are welcome here."

Having established the need and calling of the church, in 8:1-3, Luke pointed out that the early church fulfilled that need by providing a place of welcome to women from various backgrounds. Acceptance and love was the calling of the church of Jesus Christ — acceptance and love of the despised centurion, acceptance and love of the abandoned and dependent widow.

It was acceptance and love of the woman who was a sinner and all women who had been disenfranchised and left out, rejected and lied to because of their reputation.

Acceptance and love.

This was the calling of the church of Jesus Christ and all who called themselves members of that body.

Proper 7

Luke 8:26-39

The Call To Encounter

> As he stepped out on land, a man of the city who had demons met him. For a long time, he had worn no clothes, and he did not live in a house but in the tombs. When he saw Jesus, he fell down before him and shouted at the top of his voice, "What have you to do with me, Jesus, Son of the Most High God? I beg you, do not torment me..." Jesus then asked him, "What is your name?" He said, "Legion"; for many demons had entered him. They begged him not to order them to go back into the abyss.
>
> Luke 8: 27-31

To Gerasa

Picture the Sea of Galilee in your mind.

Capernaum was at about ten o'clock and the town of Gerasa, the country of the Gerasenes, would have been at about five o'clock.

Jesus and his disciples had visited Capernaum, a Jewish city, and the towns and villages around it, healing, teaching and preaching, but the crowds were getting too big and maybe a little out of control, so Jesus said, "Let's go somewhere else. Somewhere across the lake." They climbed in their boats and off they went. We don't know where they were headed, but they ran into a storm, which Jesus quieted, and they ended up landing near the town of Gerasa, home of the Gerasenes.

The Gerasenes are Gentiles, not Jews, and Luke's audience probably caught their collective breath as they heard this because you never knew what those Gentiles were going to do; how they were going to react to or treat Jews.

A common reaction to "the other," is it not?

Our sons and daughters grow up and say they want to be missionaries and go to a foreign land to help the helpless and, admit it, parents, our first response is, "You want to help people, fine. But aren't there some people right here at home you can help? Some poor people, some hungry people, some needy people right here, not just in America, but right here in Ohio? Why do you have to go way over there?"

And if that doesn't work, maybe we pull out the old rumor mill. "You know what I heard about those people..." We try to scare them out of going because, well, those people...

I guess it's a natural thing. We want our kids to be near so we can see them and be with them. We want them to be safe and happy. It seems most reasonable to us that safe and happy would be right here, close to us.

But there's also, in our response, just a plain, old, common fear of anything that is different or new or odd, a fear of the foreign, the distant, the alien, the peculiar. Given the opportunity, we will spend all our time comfortably ensconced within our own group — people who look like, sound like, talk like, and eat like us.

Jesus had different ideas, though.

The gospel, it seems, is for all people. Color and culture mattered not a whit to him. And maybe it shouldn't to us, if we want to be his disciples. Maybe we can learn from those who are different from us. Important stuff, sure, but fun stuff, too.

Recently I discovered a band called Ranky Tanky that plays modern riffs on traditional Gullah music that originated in the low country of South Carolina (below Charleston). When I heard of the band, I was curious about their music because I had visited the low country on a mission trip and was introduced to the Gullah culture, music, and, well, food, of course. The band's name is apropos because that's what the music sounds like. It's kind of Ranky Tanky, and I never would have been able to enjoy it if I had not left my comfort zone and visited another culture.

The Demoniac

Not only did Jesus call us, through his example, to encounter other cultures than our own, he called us to encounter individual people who are different from us.

No sooner had he and his disciples placed their feet on dry land than they were confronted by this man who was, well, let's just say it, crazy as a bedbug. Back then they called it demonic possession but, today, we would more likely call it mental illness. In this case, accompanied by some form of seizure disorder, maybe we would call it epilepsy.

He didn't wear clothing, he lived in the cemetery, he ran around accosting people with gibberish, he flailed about, hurting himself and possibly causing harm to others. So out of control was he that the people in the town had marshalled their strong men to chain him to a rock to keep him from doing damage to himself or others. But he was so strong, and made stronger by his illness, that he broke the chains.

They were at their wits' end.

So, he ran up to Jesus, fell on the ground, and begged Jesus to leave him alone.

Jesus recognized that there was more at work, here, than just some weird behavior and he directly addressed the demon that had possessed the man, asking his name.

It was believed, in the first century, that knowing a person's name gave one a certain power over that person. It's not unlike how we differentiate between given names, nicknames, and formal names. If someone refers to me as Dean, but expects me to refer to her as Mrs. _____, that indicates a power differential, doesn't it? Or if I insist that members of my church refer to me as Reverend Feldmeyer while I call all of them by nick-names that I have made up for them, what am I saying about where the power lies in our relationship?

So, Jesus wanted to know the name of the demon, but...

Turns out there was more than one demon and they answered in unison, "Legion" which can mean a thousand or just, many, and can just as easily be translated "mob." We weren't told how many but we were told that this guy had a bunch of problems.

Sound familiar?

The problems that assail us rarely come one at a time, do they? Hence the old axiom, "When it rains, it pours."

This is often the case with problems that originate within us as with problems that originate from outside ourselves. I make a mistake and I get angry about it and my anger causes me to make a second mistake, which only multiplies my frustration, which causes me to make yet a third mistake, at which I throw up my hands and storm out of the room to come back later when I've cooled off.

I've learned from mental health professionals that this is often the case with those who suffer from mental illness. Often, one type of mental illness can bring on another. It is not uncommon for people with schizophrenia, for instance, to also be depressed or people with borderline personality disorder to also have narcissistic personality disorder as well.

So, how did Jesus deal with this legion of demons that possessed this poor man and had been torturing him for a long, long time?

Oddly, enough, he employed mercy.

The Swine And The Swineherds

The person with the illness stepped back into the wings and the affliction, itself, took center stage with Jesus as they conversed.

The affliction knew that Jesus held all the power in this situation and could, if he chose, fling it back into the pit or abyss from which it came so the affliction begged Jesus for mercy. "Please don't send us back to the pit," they said and, seeing a herd of swine grazing on a nearby hillside, they asked him to let them enter the pigs.

Remember, to first-century Jews, pigs are unclean, worthless animals not unlike groundhogs or muskrats would be to us. No matter that some people actually enjoy eating groundhogs and collecting the pelts of muskrats for sale, we consider them creepy and disgusting and that's the way Luke's audience would have seen these pigs. A first-century Jewish audience would have no ethical problems with destroying a herd of pigs so a person could be saved from a self-destructive mental illness.

Jesus gave the demons permission to enter the herd of swine and the pigs, immediately, stampeded over the nearby cliff and ran headlong into the sea where they were drowned and, presumably, the demons were drowned as well as their host died and they had no other into which they could escape.

Jesus was merciful to the evil ones, giving them that for which they asked and they were, nevertheless, destroyed. Evil is destructive, and nothing can change that. It destroys that which it inhabits and, thus, defines its own destruction.

The focus shifted from the corpses of the pigs, bobbing on the surf, to the swineherds whose pigs these were or who, at the very least, were being paid to tend them. They ran back to the city and the surrounding countryside to tell what they had just experienced.

We can imagine that their eagerness to tell what happened may have had any number of motivations. They may have wanted to make sure their boss knew that it wasn't their fault that his pigs were all dead. Or, if the pigs belonged to them, they may have wanted to report Jesus for stampeding them over the cliff, thus depriving them of their livelihood. Or, maybe they just wanted to tell everyone about this really cool thing they had just seen, a new guy in town, exorcising a whole bunch of spirits out of the Crazy Old Dave out at the cemetery and allowing them to take up residence in some pigs, who immediately committed suicide. Now is that a story to tell or what?

At any rate, and for whatever the reason, they related their story to the townspeople who turned out in droves. This is an image worth holding onto for the next few minutes, however, as we will be coming back to it as an example of one kind of witness as compared to another which is to come.

The People Of The Town And Country

The people of the town and surrounding countryside were overcome with curiosity and make their way out to the seaside. There they discovered Jesus and, sitting at his feet, the man from the cemetery now fully dressed and perfectly sane.

Again, the ones who had seen it, presumably, the swineherds

and some others who happened to be in attendance attest to what they saw, how the afflicted man was healed by Jesus. And, in response, all the people from the city and countryside congratulated the formerly afflicted man and celebrated with him about his newly realized sanity and...

Oh, no, wait... That wasn't what happened, was it?

No, what happened was they realized that some kind of very big power was at work there and it scared them, so they told Jesus and his disciples to take a hike. Get out. Please leave and don't let the door hit you on the way out.

I like the way Eugene Peterson put it in The Message. "Later, a great many people from the Gerasene countryside got together and asked Jesus to leave — too much change, too fast, and they were scared."

These folks would be more comfortable with one of their own suffering horrible mental illness than with a sudden change that might cure him.

Been there, seen that — right?

One of my ministerial mentors once told me, when I was first starting out in the ministry, "If you want to make some changes in the church, always put those things at the beginning of the meeting." And he was right. I soon learned that people tend to accept an arbitrary number of changes after which they begin to get very uncomfortable and even scared. It is as though a few changes are okay, but if you approve too many, things will get out of hand and out of control and the next thing you know, *chaos*!

It's not a rational thing. It's a feeling like when you run down a hill and before long you are going too fast to stop and you know that a crash is eminent. You do crash and fall down and your mother comes and dusts you off and puts a Band-aid on your knee and says, "See? I told you, you were going too fast."

There is a story of a young minister who preached in a church that had, at one time in its history, had a central pulpit but many years ago, another pastor had divided the chancel with a lectern on one side and the pulpit on the other.

One day, soon after his arrival, the new, young pastor removed the lectern and put the pulpit back in the center of the chancel where it had originally been, many years ago. The congregation threw a fit. How dare he make such a radical change?

So, he put it back over to the side and, the next Sunday he moved it one inch toward the center. A month later he moved it another inch. A month later, another inch and so on and so on until it was in the center and no one ever noticed the change.

I once served a church with the American flag in the center of the chancel. Thinking that the center of worship should be God, I moved the flag to the side of the chancel, with the Christian flag on the opposite side.

A few months later, I moved the flags to the opposite sides, not of the chancel, but of the nave. And, a year later, I removed them altogether from the sanctuary. It was five years later that someone finally noticed.

Sometimes Jesus calls us to incremental change but, sometimes, incremental change is just another way of saying, "slow death." Sometimes Jesus calls us to quick and abrupt change. There can be no slow incremental change from racism to equality, from hate to love, from greed to generosity. These are immediate, fast, and total changes that Jesus requires of everyone who would call themselves his disciples. That brings us back to the man formerly known as "demoniac."

Formerly Known As The Demoniac

Jesus didn't go to Gerasa looking for trouble. He came there for the same reason he went anywhere: to spread God's good news of grace and acceptance and reconciliation and love. And he did so with the afflicted man.

But they wanted him to leave because they were afraid of the demands of the gospel. And he did.

Just as he was getting into the boat, the man he healed came running up and asked to go along with him and be a disciple.

Wouldn't it be cool if Jesus had said "Yes?" Wouldn't that just complete this story in the nicest way, tying up the loose ends in a neat bow? Sorry, not this time.

"No," Jesus told the man. "You need to stay here and tell

everyone what God has done for you."

In other words, go be a witness to God's activity and power in your life. Unlike the swineherds who witness to what they saw, this man witnesses to what he experienced. He tells his story. He goes out into the world that he knows, the gentile world, not the foreign mission field, but his own hometown, and he tells his story.

And when you get right down to it, isn't that all that any of us has when it comes to making our witness — our own story?

Has your life been renewed in some way by the love of God?

Tell the story.

Have you found yourself with new life after you were accepted by God when others rejected you?

Tell the story.

Did you find new meaning and purpose in the fellowship of your church?

Tell the story.

Were you at your wit's end when some other person lifted you up and showed you that there was hope? Tell the story.

Our most effective witness is not when we knock on the doors of strangers or when we shout through a bullhorn on a street corner, or even when we erect billboards or hire skywriters. Our most effective witness is when, at the right time, in the right place, to the right person, in the right way, we tell our story. Amen.

Proper 8

Luke 9:51-62

The Art Of Transition

> Another said, "I will follow you, Lord; but let me first say farewell to those at my home." Jesus said to him, "No one who puts a hand to the plow and looks back is fit for the kingdom of God."
>
> Luke 9:61-62

Someone once said that people do not voluntarily change until their level of discomfort is greater than their level of fear.

I have a good friend, a fellow baby-boomer, who was required by the company he worked for to move to a different part of the state. The move meant a promotion and a sizable raise in his pay, but he was ambivalent about it. His kids were in middle school and had friends they'd have to leave. He and his wife were active in the church and the schools. While he looked forward to the new challenges of his job, he was sad about all that he would be losing in the move. He shared that sadness and ambivalence with me one day over lunch. There was a long pause in the conversation and he shrugged and said, "But change is good."

Later, as I recalled that conversation, I thought that our generation, the baby-boomers were probably the first generation in American history who believed that change was a good thing for its own sake.

For most of us, change does not come easily or gently. It is not something that we eagerly embrace; it is forced upon us. We go into it kicking and screaming. We age. Our bodies change. People we know and care about move away. We change jobs and have to learn new skills and face new responsibilities. Our doctor tells us we have to change our eating and exercise habits.

Even the changes we seek cause us distress and discomfort.

That new baby we wanted so much keeps us up at night with feedings and worry and continues to do so for the rest of her life, at least the worry part. We finally get to retire and then we find ourselves feeling bored and forgotten. The new easy chair turns out to be less comfortable than the old one. The new computer means I have to learn a lot of stuff that I got along fine without knowing yesterday.

Life doesn't ask our permission before it changes, however. If we are going to have authentic and effective lives, we must find a way to deal with the changes that life, and the gospel, requires of us.

A Changing World

Looking back, we should have known that, sooner or later, an epidemic would come and threaten us. Even a casual glance at history shows that to be the case. Truth be told, we were overdue. We dodged the bullet on the swine flu and the bird flu. Yeah, we should have seen it coming. We should have been prepared.

Yet, when the coronavirus did come, it took us by surprise.

Looking back, we should have known that those levies would eventually fail. They were made by hand; too short, too thin, and too fragile. If the right hurricane came at the right time in the right place, they would not be able to contain the storm surge and New Orleans would be devastated.

Yet, when Katrina came, she took us by surprise.

Looking back, we probably should have known that the economy couldn't continue to grow the way it was growing, based, as it was, on sub-prime mortgages and financial manipulations that most of us couldn't even pronounce, much less understand.

Yet, when things went south, it took us by surprise.

Looking back, we probably should have known that a huge oil spill was inevitable and been prepared for such an eventuality. Those wells are a mile below the surface of the ocean, where the water pressure is over a ton per square inch. We should have known and been prepared.

Yet, when the BP blowout came in the Gulf of Mexico, it took us by surprise.

These tragedies and others all took us by surprise and they have forced changes upon us that have taken us by surprise as well.

I remember when flying on an airplane was exciting and fun. 9/11 changed all that, didn't it? Now an airline flight is like a trial by ordeal; it's something you have to endure to get where you want or need to go. And the rules for flying are constantly changing. A year ago, you couldn't take even a nail file on board an airplane. This month the nail file is fine, but you can't get a tube of toothpaste through security. Oh, and now you have to wear a mask.

The only way most of us can endure the airline ordeal is to stay focused on the destination. "Yes, this is torture," we say to ourselves. "But in just a couple of hours I'll be in Las Vegas, or Sarasota, or Corpus Christi..." or wherever.

We knew our kids were getting older but we weren't quite prepared for them to move out, start living lives of their own, and forgetting to call us for days on end. We knew that our parents were getting older, but we weren't quite prepared for them to slow down the way they have and become so dependent upon us. We knew that we were getting older but... well, you know.

No matter how much change we experience, it always takes us by surprise. If we are not careful, the changes that fall upon us can distract us from our destinations — the visions we had of our future and the goals we had set for our lives.

And change is coming at us faster and faster. Look what has happened in just the last forty years:

The first personal computer, the IBM 5150 came on the market in 1981. By 2008, there were one billion personal computers in homes around the world and that number doubled in 2015. And most of those computers are capable of doing lots more than we ask of them.

In 1993, there were 600 "www" web sites. By 1997 there were over a million. By 2005 the number had grown to about 71 million. And while there is no way to know for sure, the best estimates for today run in the neighborhood of about 200 million. That's an increase of more than 300,000% in less than thirty years.

The first email message was sent in 1971, but it didn't become popular until 1988 and today more than 600 million people use email regularly. Most scholars consider it to be the most important development in communication technology since the telephone.

Speaking of telephones, text messaging wasn't available to most people until 1993. Twitter wasn't available until 2006. Both of them have become part of our everyday lives. My colleagues, who are younger than me, insist that texting is not just part of their life; it is an essential part if they want to stay in touch with their kids.

(Oh, and a footnote: I remember, ten years ago, when I first typed the word "texting" on my then nine-year-old computer it told me that "texting" wasn't a word.)

Many of us have gone from playing our parents' 72 rpm records to playing our own 45's through vinyl albums, to eight-tracks, to cassettes, to CDs to MP3s to streaming music on our phones.

And nobody, you will notice, asked our permission or even our opinion before making these changes. How are we supposed to live with them?

The Word

In the gospel lesson, Luke showed how Jesus refused to be distracted from his calling and his goal. He set his face toward Jerusalem and, despite distractions, refused to be diverted.

Change, while inevitable, can also be a distraction, however. It can, if we are not careful, divert us from the work of the kingdom. The gospel of Jesus Christ reminds us that we are called to be transformed by God's grace and not to settle simply for being changed by the world. We must be constantly on our guard to not confuse the two.

Distracted By Our Own Reactivity

In the first example, Jesus and his disciples were rejected by the Samaritans and his disciples got their feelings hurt and wanted to stop and get some revenge. They wanted to bring down fire and brimstone on these heathens and an astute student of the Bible recognized this as a direct reference to the prophet, Elijah who destroyed some soldiers who scoffed at his calling.

The disciples wanted Jesus to do the same thing to the Samaritans. Show them you are a true prophet of God, they said. Do what Elijah did. Bring down fire to destroy these guys.

Jesus rebuked them. Elijah's way of doing things was no longer appropriate. We are starting a new order and a new way of being and relating to God and our neighbor, a way based on grace, love, kindness, and generosity.

How easy it is to be diverted from the kingdom, especially by the acts of other people, their reactions to us and our reactions to their reactions. We take disagreements personally. We are insulted by anyone who has another view, another idea, another way of doing things.

These days it is rare to hear two people discuss differing points of view without raining fire and brimstone on each other. The well-modulated, rational discussion has become a thing of the past, a cliché, as we bombard each other with verbal fire and brimstone, axioms, sound bites, accusations, and denunciations.

Rabbi and psychologist Edwin Friedman reminded us that, "The first responsibility of a leader," he said, "is to be the non-anxious presence in an anxious system." But then he reminded us that, "all systems are, by nature, anxious, and they will, inevitably, accuse anyone who doesn't join them in their anxiety of being distant, cold, uncaring, and even cruel."[9]

True leaders do not allow themselves to be distracted by accusations and denunciations from detractors but keep their eyes focused with laser-like intensity on the vision and the goal which lies ahead.

Distracted By Comfort

The second distraction which Jesus offered up is that of comfort, especially the comforts associated with hearth and

9 A Failure of Nerve: Leadership in the Age of the Quick Fix by Edwin Friedman.

home: ease, reassurance, safety, and familiarity.

The man came up to Jesus and said, "I will follow you wherever you go."

And Jesus seemed to reply, "Good, because that's exactly where I'm going...*wherever*."

Wherever the gospel calls us to go, we go. Wherever the need is profound, we go. Wherever the good news has not been heard, we go. Wherever the hungry are not fed, the naked are not clothed, the thirsty are not quenched, the pained are not given comfort, the sick and imprisoned are not visited, to those places, we go.

Those are the places we are called by Jesus to go, brothers and sisters. And there isn't one of them that fits neatly into most of our comfort zones. They call us out of our La-Z-Boy's. They require us to leave the streets with which we are familiar and drive in the city or on the freeway. They shove us into the sick rooms, the visiting rooms, the soup kitchens, the breadlines, the jails and prisons, and the slums where no sane person voluntarily goes.

This discipleship business, this life in the kingdom of God, is not for weaklings, whiners, or complainers. There is no room for drama, or narcissism, for the easily bruised, or the slow to heal.

Jesus said it clearly, folks. Wild animals have it easier than those who choose to be his disciples. We cannot let ourselves by distracted by our need for comfort, reassurance, safety, and familiarity.

Distracted By Responsibility

The second man who came to Jesus said he wanted to follow Jesus but, first, he had to bury his father.

I used to think that this meant that his father was already dead and he just had to go to the funeral. But we know that what the guy was saying was that he had an elderly parent that required looking after. As soon as the old man died, however, look out, we're gonna get our discipleship on.

He said that he wanted to follow Jesus, he wanted to be a true disciple, just not right now. He had too many other responsibilities. But later, oh, later he's going to set the world on fire with his devotion.

Later, after the kids have moved out and the dog has died...

Later, after mom and dad die or at least move into the nursing home...

Later, after I get my retirement all set in stone and paid for...

After my wife and I have had a chance to talk...

After I've discharged all my responsibilities at the lodge...

After, after, after... after everything *else* is taken care of, then I'll have time to actually become a real disciple of Jesus Christ. But for now, I'll just hang around at the edges, pick up some pointers now and then, write a few checks, be a basically good and decent person, and that will have to suffice.

Let me be clear: *There's nothing wrong with being a basically good and decent person.* There's nothing wrong with taking care of your elderly parents, your kids, your dog, your retirement. In fact, what we discover in all these examples that Luke was leading us through this morning, is that none of them are bad.

None of them are wrong. They are all good things, nice things, decent things.

Luke's point, however, was that we can be led away from the kingdom of God, we can be distracted and diverted from that path which leads to authentic life by the good things as easily as we can by the bad. In fact, given the opportunity, Satan will almost always choose good things, nice things, decent things as his weapons of choice. We do not need to choose the evil or the bad for Satan to triumph; the lesser good will do nicely, thank you.

The kingdom of God is often as much about prioritizing goods as it about choosing between goods and evils. We who choose to live life in God's kingdom cannot let ourselves be distracted and diverted from that path by the little goods that lead us away from the great ones.

Distracted By Convention

The third man wanted to follow Jesus but first he wanted to go home say goodbye to his family, presumably, his parents and siblings. (Not a bad thing, right?)

Here we are, once again, hurled back to the Hebrew scriptures. This is another direct reference to Elijah and his protégé, Elisha. In the nineteenth chapter of 1 Kings, Elijah chose Elisha out of a field of farm workers to be his successor. Elisha agreed, but he asked if he could first go home and say goodbye to his parents. He realized that this was going to be a clean break. He would never be able to go back, to unring the bell he was about to ring.

Elijah allowed him to go back and say goodbye, which he did by killing the oxen he was using to plow with and roasting them over a fire made from the wooden plow. He gave the meat to his family and their hired hands, kissed his parents and left.

Jesus said that this was exactly the kind of break that was needed to become a Disciple (capital D). We cannot move forward if we keep one foot always in the past. We cannot look forward and backward at the same time. Our gaze must be focused only upon that which lies ahead, upon the vision God has given to us and the goals that have arisen from that vision.

And perhaps a quick, but important word should be said, here, about parents.

There is no getting around the fact that in two of the illustrations Luke provided, the biggest obstacles to living the life of discipleship were parents. It is we parents who constantly remind our children that they really do owe it to us to be safe and happy.

We sometimes fail to remember that what God calls us to, often leads us through brief, acute periods of danger, discomfort, and unhappiness so that we can later experience higher and more complete levels of true joy in him. In other words, we parents are often huge parts of that past with which our children must break in order to become authentic disciples of Jesus Christ. And it is only after that break has been cleanly made that they can return to us as friends.

Then we can walk together in the path of discipleship.

A New Kind Of Discipleship

In today's gospel lesson, Luke bookends the four stories with thinly veiled references to the change which occurred in the nature of prophecy when the mantel was passed from Elijah to Elisha. Just as the meaning of prophecy changed then, so Jesus changed the meaning of discipleship some 800 years later.

Up until this story, a disciple was simply someone who followed a teacher around and learned from him. The primary activity of a disciple was simply taking notes.

Here Jesus changed that. He upped the ante. He raised the bar.

Discipleship, at least for those who would be disciples of Jesus Christ, no longer had just to do with learning stuff from the teacher, it has to do with *being like* the teacher. It has to do not just with changing our minds, but with transforming our lives.

Discipleship is about transformation of the entire soul — the heart, the mind, the body — the whole shootin' works. And as disciples, we are called to ask and search diligently those new things which are placed before us, to determine which are transforming our lives and which are simply changing them. Amen.

Proper 9

Luke 10:1-11, 16-20

As A Fire Exists By Burning

> After this the Lord appointed seventy others and sent them on ahead of him in pairs to every town and place where he himself intended to go. He said to them, "The harvest is plentiful, but the laborers are few; therefore, ask the Lord of the harvest to send out laborers into his harvest. Go on your way. See, I am sending you out like lambs into the midst of wolves. Luke 10:1-3

> "The church exists by mission as fire exists by burning." Emil Brunner

Groundhog Day In West Virginia

Years ago, some other adults and I took the youth group from our church on a mission trip to the Appalachia Service Project in West Virginia.

My team consisted of me, an adult woman, and eight kids, aged 13-18. We were sent to a little house, built on a shelf cut into the steep side of a large hill. Whoever built the house had not taken into account the effect of the erosion caused by rainwater running down the hill and around the house, which was going to wash off the side of the hill if something wasn't done.

Our job was to dig a French drain that would channel the rainwater around the house and down the hill. We were also to rebuild the front porch, which stood on pillars of stacked stones that were in danger of toppling over, and to make other repairs that the owner wished done.

The owner was Mrs. Davis, a short, round, jolly, loving, elderly lady who came out to greet us every morning and always provided us with fresh, cold, spring water in the heat of the day.

One day, our work was interrupted by a heavy thunderstorm around lunchtime and we all came up onto the big porch that we had, that morning, finished reinforcing. The lady of the house came out and, seeing us eating our sack lunches, said, "Y'all should have come on in. I woulda cooked somethin' up for ya."

We all declared how that would have been nice of her but absolutely unnecessary. Our banter went back and forth for a while and one of the kids asked her, "What would you have cooked for us, Mrs. Davis?"

"Well, I mighta fried up a couple of them chickens, yonder," she said, pointing to the chickens running around her tiny yard. "Or I mighta pulled a groundhog outa the freezer and roasted it up with some onions and taters."

All talk came to a screeching halt as everyone turned to see if she was kidding. When the silence threatened to go uncomfortably long, I asked, "Mrs. Davis, do you really have a groundhog in your deep freezer?"

"More'n one," she said. "My boy shoots 'em and cleans 'em up and brings 'em over. You wanna see?"

I certainly did, and she led me to the deep freezer on the back porch of the house and opened the lid and, sure enough, there were some frozen animals in there, each about the size of a large football. I couldn't swear that they were groundhogs, but I couldn't swear they weren't.

"Y'all ain't never ate groundhog before, have ya?" she asked us, laughing and looking around at the kids standing there with their mouths agape. We all allowed that we had not.

"Well, tomorrow you're gonna. You just come on back here and for lunch, you're gonna have the best groundhog ever cooked in these hills." We all agreed that we would, indeed, return and that we were all looking forward to a new gastronomic adventure.

Except, of course, we *all* weren't. Several of the kids were turning green at the thought of eating groundhog and, to tell the truth, I may have, too, if Mrs. Davis hadn't nudged me on the arm as we filed off the porch and motioned for me to bend down to hear her speak softly. She whispered to me, "Tastes like roast pork. Just a little gamier."

The next morning, our last of the week, as we gathered around the cars to make our way to Mrs. Davis's house, I delivered a small lecture to our group about being good guests. It didn't take much talking as the Appalachian Service Project had already pounded it into our heads that we were guests in those hills and should be on our best behavior at all times.

I made it clear that "best behavior" included not turning up our noses at the food that was offered to us and, at least, trying a taste of everything that was provided. Smile, no matter what you really think. And say *thank you* like you mean it.

When we arrived at her house, Mrs. Davis was nearly giddy with anticipation. Her son, daughter-in-law, and two grandchildren had come to help with the big meal and she had brought out her best of everything. Sawhorses had been set up and boards laid across them for tables with handmade quilts spread over the boards as tablecloths. The dishes were of all kinds and patterns, some hers and some her son's. It was the same with the flatware. Drinking glasses included Mason jars and Flintstone jelly glasses. Our beverage was lemonade made from cold spring water and the chairs were of every kind imaginable.

The meal went well. The kids took a little of everything that was offered. Cornbread, groundhog smothered in onions (it did taste like roasted pulled pork, only a little gamier), roasted potatoes, carrots, and corn on the cob. We all might have eaten more, but the house wasn't air conditioned and it had to be about 100 degrees in that living room. As it was, we talked, ate,laughed, and thanked Mrs. Davis profusely and the meal went on for more than an hour in the sweltering heat.

Then, just as I was starting to tell everyone that it was time to get back to work, Mrs. Davis stopped me. "Y'all haven't had my special dessert," she said, winking at her daughter-in-law and smiling a huge smile. She disappeared into the kitchen for a few minutes and returned with a pan fresh off the stove, the contents of which she was slowly and carefully folding with a big spoon.

Without a word of explanation, she handed it to the lady who was my fellow chaperone. Debbie looked in the pan, patted her stomach and said, thanks, but she was full, just couldn't eat another bite or she'd explode. Coward — she passed the pan to the next person.

Same reaction several times: Look in the pan. Make a doubtful face. Pass the pan along.

Inevitably, the pan came to me. I took it, looked into it, and I could see why their reactions had been what they were. There was a glob of something about two or three inches thick in the bottom of the pan. It was sorta purple and, well, the only word I could think of at the time was "slimy" looking. It didn't smell bad, kinda sweet and fruity, but it looked awful. I didn't blame the kids who had demurred on dessert. My admonition to be a good guest could be pushed only so far.

As the deliverer of the lecture, however, I figured I didn't have a choice.

I took the spoon, scooped up a medium size dollop of the purple and white stuff, whatever it was, and put it on my plate. I passed the pan on and time stood still while everyone watched me taste Mrs. Davis's special dessert.

I took a modest portion on my spoon, raised it slowly to my face, blew on it to cool it a bit, and then, in one quick movement, slipped it into my mouth.

It was delicious.

Mrs. Davis saw my smile and finally explained: She and her grandchildren had gone out that spring and picked wild raspberries and blueberries, brought them home and froze them. This morning, she had boiled some of them in sugar water until she had a thick syrup then dropped biscuit dough into the syrup making berry dumplings.

To the untrained eye, they looked kind of, well, slimy. But once I knew what they were, I took another helping and announced to the group that dessert was the best part of the meal. Mrs. Davis clapped her hands in front of her face, which was nearly bursting with joy and pride.

A couple of the kids in our group took a helping of the dessert and pronounced it good.

We all agreed that we were much too full to go back to work. The crew from the following week would have to finish up the tasks we had begun. We spent the rest of the afternoon sitting in the shade. I had brought my old campfire guitar and we sang some songs and swapped stories. The kids in our group played soccer with Mrs. Davis's grandkids.

Finally, we packed up the tools, which had seen only modest use that day, passed around hugs and handshakes, then bid our hosts farewell.

On our first night in West Virginia, at the orientation meeting for the adult leaders, our ASP leader had said something like this: Appalachia Service Project is not a home building or home repair ministry. There are cheaper, easier ways to do home building and repair than by using a bunch of city teenagers who have to be trained how to use a saw and hammer. ASP is a ministry of Christian witness and we make that witness through the relationships we build while we're doing home repair. We're here to build Christian relationships and maybe a house or two."

Even as I say these words to you, I can see Mrs. Davis clapping her hands and smiling as big as you please, as I tasted her berry dumplings and pronounced them delicious.

But, you ask, what does that have to do with today's lesson from Luke's gospel?

Company's Comin'

There are some New Testament scholars who insist that we can't possibly understand the full meaning of the synoptic gospels (Matthew, Mark, and Luke) unless we study them in the context of the first Jewish War that took place from 66-73 CE. I concur.

This is a sermon, not a history lecture, so I'll try to keep the contextualizing short, but please do not equate brevity with unimportance. This stuff is important if we want to take seriously our understanding of the gospels.

In 66 CE, about thirty years after the first Easter, two factions of insurgent Israeli guerilla fighters (what the Romans would have called terrorists) joined together to start a rebellion to throw off their Roman oppressors.

Those two factions were the Zealots and a splinter group called the Sicarii. You are probably familiar with the Zealots as they are mentioned in the gospels and it is from them that we get the word "zealous." The lesser known Sicarii derived their name from the *sicae,* small daggers they concealed in their garments. Their favorite tactic was to blend into large gatherings and use the hidden daggers to kill Romans or those who they deemed Roman sympathizers and then get away by blending back into the crowd.

The Sicarii were regarded as the earliest known organized, cloak and dagger style assassination group, predating the Islamic Hashishin and Japanese ninja by centuries. The Spanish term *sicario* is used in contemporary Latin America to describe a hitman working for a drug cartel.

The Sicarii split with the Zealots because they believed the Zealots were too political and not ruthless enough to seize their independence from the Romans, but the two groups rejoined for the First Jewish War.

After some initial success by the rebels, the Romans, brought in battle hardened legions, attacking simultaneously from land to the north and from the sea to the west.

The war lasted a total of seven years and resulted in the destruction of Jerusalem and the Jewish temple, as well as widespread destruction throughout Judea. Historians believe that more than 6,000 Jews were killed in the city of Jerusalem alone and somewhere around 1.2 million throughout all of Palestine, many by the Sicarii, who assassinated anyone who tried to surrender or flee, but mostly by the Romans. The war ended with the mass suicide of 960 souls, Zealots and their families, at the fortress at Masada.

The war also resulted in a permanent schism between Judaism and early Christianity and the consolidation of non-messianic Jewish groups into Rabbinic Judaism, the center of which became

Galilee.

It is also widely believed that over a million Jews and Jewish Christians fled Judea south to Egypt and North to Syria (Antioch) and Asia Minor (Ephesus).

The Christian communities in Ephesus and Antioch were suddenly flooded with strangers; Christians, yes, but a different kind of Christian than those to which they were accustomed. Most of the people in the Lukan Church of Antioch would have been gentiles and these newcomers were Jewish Christians.

They spoke a different language, had different customs, ate different foods, worshiped with different rituals, and were just, well, different. How could they possibly be blended into the Antiochan (Lukan) Christian community?

Much of Luke's gospel is given to answering that question. Luke believed that Jesus was the answer. It is by embodying Jesus' example that we can all learn to get along in spite of our differences. It is by hearing his message, his teaching and commandments, and watching his healing, reconciling ministry and that of the early fathers and mothers of the church in the book of Acts, that we can learn to all get along, and much of this message is directed at the Lukan church as he expected them to open their arms and hearts to the Judean refugees.

But, in today's lesson, Luke paused to talk, not to the hosts, but to the guests, the refugees, themselves, and he couched their plight in terms of mission. They had been sent, he said, on a mission to bring the good news of Jesus Christ to people different from themselves.

Rules For Guests

Luke was the only gospel writer who told this story. It had some things in common with the stories in Mark and Matthew where Jesus sent out the twelve disciples. But in Luke's mission story, the number of disciples was greater. He chose the highly symbolic and significant number: seventy.

(The number is mentioned 61 times in the Bible. Sixty times in the Hebrew scriptures and once in the New Testament.)

The number of Christian refugees who poured into Antioch

can, of course, not be known, but the number seventy indicated that it was a lot. The Antiochan Christians were expected to help them, which, by all accounts, they did. But the refugees had responsibilities too, primary the spreading of the gospel of Jesus to those who had not heard it.

Yes, the war was a terrible thing and we grieve for those who were lost, but that does not relieve us of our responsibilities as Christians any more than does a hurricane, a flood, or a pandemic. "We've a story to tell to the nations," as we used to sing in the old hymn.

We are all, in a sense, called by Jesus to go ahead of him and announce his coming.

And while we are doing so, we are to "eat what is set before" us, be it kosher or not, groundhog or berry dumpling that, upon first inspection, looks suspiciously slimy. Food is now, as it was then, the very stuff of life and it reminds us that we are all dependent. The most important events in our lives are celebrated with food. We gather at the table at Christmas, Thanksgiving, Easter, after funerals and weddings, and at baptisms. We celebrate the Lord's presence with us at a symbolic holy meal that we call "communion," literally, "becoming one."

So, when someone places food before you, honor it with openness and gratitude, Jesus instructed then and now.

Three other admonitions among the many that Jesus speaks to his seventy disciples and Luke to the refugees who had descended upon Antioch, require our brief attention before we are quit of this pericope.

Note, please, that two marks of true, Christian evangelists are vulnerability and dependency. The disciples are going out into the mission field as sheep among wolves, vulnerable and open. They were to be dependent upon the kindness and generosity and the hospitality of their hosts. They were not to shop around for better accommodations or provisions.

While we and our families have not taken a vow of poverty, neither have we taken up the cross of Christ to cash in on it. We are to take no more than we need and accept what is provided for us with gratitude.

I'm not talking just about the clergy, here. In this passage, Jesus and Luke called us to know the difference in what we need and what we want and to make that difference real and meaningful in our lives. To do so is a witness in and of itself. By our example we can carry a message to the whole world about what is and is not truly necessary and important.

Finally, Luke used the words of Jesus to warn us against judging others, especially those who do not accept our preaching or our Lord.

Professor Fred Craddock pointed out that in this passage, "Rituals of departure were to be brief, leaving such persons to be judged by what they had missed — that is, the kingdom of God had been near." (*Interpretation: A Bible Commentary for Teaching and Preaching; Luke*. Fred B. Craddock. P. 145.)

If a judgment is to come, it will come from Jesus at a later time. As for us, upon our departure, we are to speak the same words to those who do not accept our message as we do to those who do accept it: "The kingdom of God has come near." The basic message, says Craddock, is "not contingent upon the response."

Sisters and brothers, we are all refugees, resident aliens, fleeing the past we left behind when we first heard God's good news and were called to spread that good news to the whole world. Spread it first in our families, then in our communities, then our regions, and beyond. Maybe even to West Virginia.

We do so through words, yes, telling our stories, but through acts also — acts of kindness, of generosity, of compassion, and care. We do so through hospitality, how we offer it to others, and how we receive it when it is offered to us.

May God grant us all the grace to make a faithful witness to the grace and love of Jesus in all that we do and say. Amen.

Proper 10

Luke 10:25-37

Why Pass By?

> But wanting to justify himself, he asked Jesus, "And who is my neighbor?" Luke 10:29

Why didn't they stop?

Why did they pass by?

One was a priest and one was a Levite, a member of the priestly class. Their high status was that of the holiest, most revered men in their community. It wasn't that they didn't see him there, bleeding, perhaps moaning, dying by the side of the road. That is made clear in the story. They saw him and, intentionally passed by on the other side.

Why?

Why did they pass by?

Maybe They Were Afraid

In the 1961 movie, *King of Kings,* there is, near the beginning of the film, a scene that looks very much like this one, at first.

We are shown a road. It is dusty, sunbaked, and hot. A man is lying at the edge of the road. He is bleeding and moaning, barely able to move. Several Roman soldiers come down the road and, after conferring with each other, they stop and go to the man to see if they can help him.

One of the soldiers knelt down and bent over the wounded man, then turned him onto his back to assess the extent of his wounds. The wounded man's eyes suddenly opened and he pulled a dagger out of his cloak and stabbed the soldier to death. Immediately, armed men leapt from behind the surrounding rocks to scrub and overwhelm the other two soldiers, killing them both. They stole the soldiers' swords and money, then disappeared into the wilderness as quickly as they appeared.

A few minutes later in the film, we learned that those were Zealots, most probably the Sicarii, fanatical ultra-violent, merciless, Jewish insurgents who had vowed to fight the Romans until the oppressors left Judea or all of the Sicarii were dead.

Apparently, this tactic was a common one not just of political terrorists but of common thieves as well.

So, maybe the priest and the Levite were just afraid for their own safety.

The Jericho Road, upon which they were traveling, was a notoriously dangerous road to travel, especially alone. Sometimes referred to as "The Blood Road" or "The Bloody Way," it was sandwiched between high cliffs on either side that kept long stretches of the road in perpetual shadow and darkness. It was a favorite haunt for thieves and highwaymen looking for an easy score and smart people did not travel it at all if they could avoid doing so and if they had to, they traveled in large groups. Anyone who did not was inviting disaster upon his or her own head.

Maybe the fear was of another type.

The man was bleeding, after all, and blood was considered a contaminant by early Jews. If you touched it or it touched you, or if you touched someone who was bleeding, you would have to have a ritual bath before you could enter the temple. You would be unclean, contaminated. Who knows what kind of diseases or infections could be lurking between those white and red blood cells.

Or maybe they were afraid they might do something wrong and make things worse. They weren't doctors, after all. They weren't trained in medicine or even first aid. What if they rolled him over and somehow made his injuries worse and he sued them.

This may have been the fear that the lawyer was experiencing who first asked Jesus, "Who is my neighbor?" What, he wanted to know, am I legally required to do? What is the minimum requirement? Is there, perhaps, a legal loophole that I can slip through that allows me to do, you know, nothing?

Theologian and popular author, Frederick Buechner, made

this observation about the story of the good samaritan in his book *Wishful Thinking* and, again, in *Beyond Words*.

"When Jesus said to love your neighbor, a lawyer who was present asked him to clarify what he meant by 'neighbor.' He wanted a legal definition of neighbor that he could refer to in case the question of loving one ever happened to come up. He presumably wanted something on the order of: 'A neighbor (hereinafter referred to as the party of the first part) is to be construed as meaning a person of Jewish descent whose legal residence is within a radius of no more than three statute miles from one's own legal residence unless there is another person of Jewish descent (hereinafter to be referred as the party of the second part) living closer to the party of the first part than one is, oneself, in which case the party of the second part is to be construed as neighbor to the party of the first part and one is oneself relieved of all responsibility of any sort or kind whatsoever.'

"Instead, Jesus told the story of the good samaritan, the point of which seemed to be that neighbor was to be construed as meaning anybody who needed you. The lawyer's response was left unrecorded."

Maybe they were just too afraid to help. They were afraid of being ambushed, by zealots, by thieves, or even by the law itself. So, they passed by.

Or, maybe they were too busy.

I'm Late, I'm Late

I'm always amused by those people who never tire of telling us how busy they are. They run here and run there, often accomplishing very little but constantly complaining about how little time they have for themselves, poor dears.

Norton Juster's wonderful, crazy, hilarious, allegorical, children's book, *The Phantom Tollbooth,* has been described as *Alice in Wonderland* on acid, and one passage in it makes a mockery of "busy" people. Young Milo, the story's protagonist, met a group of people called Lethargarians who couldn't possibly help him on his quest. Why? Because they're too busy. Busy? Doing what? Well, nothing. Nothing? Oh, yes. Doing nothing keeps us very busy, so busy we hardly have time for anything else.

"There's lots to do; we have a very busy schedule —

At 8 o'clock we get up and then we spend

From 8 to 9 daydreaming.

From 9 to 9:30 we take our early midmorning nap.

From 9:30 to 10:30 we dawdle and delay.

From 10:30 to 11:30 we take our late early morning nap.

From 11:30 to 12:00 we bide our time and then eat lunch.

From 11:00 to 2:00 we linger and loiter.

From 2:00 to 2:30 we take our early afternoon nap.

From 2:30 to 3:30 we put off for tomorrow what we could have done, today.

From 3:30 to 4:00 we take our late afternoon nap.

From 4:00 to 5:00 we loaf and lounge until dinner.

From 6:00 to 7:00 we dillydally.

From 7:00 to 8:00 we take our early evening nap and then for an hour before we go to bed at 9:00 we just waste time.

As you can see, that leaves almost no time for brooding, lagging, plodding, or procrastinating and if we stopped to think or laugh, we'd never get nothing done.

Evil Or Indifferent?

Or maybe they were just indifferent.

The late Elie Wiesel, after surviving the Auschwitz concentration camp, said that one of the most important lessons his experience taught him was that, "The opposite of love is not hate, it's indifference. The opposite of art is not ugliness, it's indifference. The opposite of faith is not heresy, it's indifference. The opposite of life is not death, it's indifference."

Perhaps these two men, the priest and the Levite, were so self-obsessed, so narcissistic, that they were simply incapable of human empathy. Maybe they could not bring themselves to care about someone they didn't know, someone whose death or survival would not affect them either way.

In the television series, "The Walking Dead," there is a scene where two of the "survivors," those who have not been infected by the deadly virus and who we know as the "good guys," are taken captive by a man who is called, "the Governor." He was the leader of another band of desperate survivors who planned to attack the good guys, kill them all, and take over their camp and their resources.

Herschel was the old man among the good guys and he was as kind, good, and decent as any character ever written for fiction. His daughters were back at the camp that the Governor intended to attack and he said to the Governor, "You are a father of a daughter. I know you love her. So how can you contemplate killing my daughters?"

The Governor steeled his face into something between a smirk and a frown and said, "They're not mine."

Maybe the priest and the Levite didn't care about the man on the side of the road because he wasn't theirs.

Or maybe they didn't stop to help him because of that lowest, most loathsome of reasons: prejudice. Maybe his skin was the wrong color, maybe his religion was not in agreement with their own, maybe his accent placed him outside the circle of their care, or maybe his income level was not sufficiently high to make him important enough. Maybe he was of the wrong political party, the wrong gender, liked the wrong music, loved the wrong person, or maybe his clothing was not sufficiently fashionable to give them pause, to convince them that he was one of them.

Maybe one of those hateful "ism's" got ahold of them and turned them aside — sexism, racism, nationalism, or ageism, classism, or... you fill in the blank.

Here is where we find the answer to how this story has survived for over 2,000 years, how it is part of our common moral mythos, regardless of our religious persuasion. Here is where we see why this story is one of the definitive stories not just of this time, but of every age.

It is a common metaphor for and a common part of our culture. How many good samaritan hospitals are there in the world, do you imagine? But while our uber-familiarity with this story may not breed contempt, it certainly often breeds defensiveness. "You can't do that in this day and age. It's too dangerous," we are told.

It doesn't matter that things were no less violent in Jesus' day.

"It isn't practical," they said, as though that, practicality, is the test of the truth of the gospel. Did you ever hear anyone, preacher or lay person, commend the teachings of Jesus on the grounds of their eminent practicality?

The truth is, many, if not most of his teachings and his commandments are hard. They're difficult. They are, not to put too fine a point on it, wholly impractical if safe, simple, and easy are what you're after.

No, let's be honest. Many of us approach this story with the attitude that, while it's a good story and we would like to be able to act in that way, we can't and so we won't and we don't.

And that's what Jesus, in telling it, and Luke, in relating it, were trying to accomplish in their listeners: attitude adjustment.

Attitude Adjustment

Most of the time, we take the wrong lesson from this story.

We hear the phrase, good samaritan, and we assume that the point of the story is that we are to accept that everyone is our neighbor regardless of their age, station, race, nationality, gender, orientation, or politics. And that's a good lesson to learn because it is, in fact the case.

It's just not the point of this story.

The point of the story is that *we can decide to be a neighbor* to anyone we choose and the way we establish that relationship is by helping them when they need help.

Who, Jesus asked, was the neighbor to this man? The injured one.

And they answered: "The one who helped him."

We become neighbors by helping each other, do you see? And how did Jesus conclude his story? "Go and do likewise." We can, in other words, decide to be a neighbor. All it takes is an attitude adjustment.

In an article on the Alban Institute website, Peter Coutts discussed the basis for his book, *Choosing Change: How to Motivate Churches to Face the Future*. He contended that it all had to do with attitude; and attitudes, he said, were made of three components:

evaluation, belief, and strength.

For many of us, we have evaluated the good samaritan's behavior as being too dangerous, too risky. This evaluation has led us to believe that we, therefore, cannot, responsibly act like the good samaritan. And that belief is made stronger every day when we read the headlines and see the reports about things like shootings and terrorism and the dangers that lurk in the shadows of the world.

So, what can we do? Too often, we have tried to change our attitudes by telling ourselves that it isn't too dangerous because God is with us and we will be "protected." Or we tell ourselves that, of course it is dangerous, but we should do it anyway because we have been in that ditch ourselves and a loving God has lifted us out of it, bandaged our moral wounds, and set us back on the road to the kingdom of God. But those rationalizations are usually ineffective because our imaginations can create endless scenarios of stopping in a bad neighborhood to help someone and being beaten, robbed, or even killed, ourselves. We leap to the worst cases scenario and it is hard to refute that it would, indeed, be dangerous under those circumstances. It would be, and, if any of us are caught in that scene. we would have some tough decisions to make.

But let's not dismiss the lesson of the good samaritan so quickly. For most of us, that scene is one that we are likely never going to face. No, the good samaritan scenario is, for most of us, going to be played out on a much smaller, simpler, and more pedestrian stage and scale.

It's going to be played out at the grocery store when we decide if we're going to let the person with only a couple of items and a cranky toddler go in front of us in the checkout line.

It's going to be played out when we have to decide whether we're going to take that close parking space or leave it for the elderly couple with the disability card hanging from their rearview mirror.

It's going to be played out when we decided if we're going to corral that grocery cart or let it roll free and possibly crash into someone's car.

It's going to be played out at school when we decide whether we're going to sit with our usual gaggle of friends in the lunchroom or maybe sit with that kid who always has to eat alone.

Once we decide to be neighbors on that scale, the scale of our everyday lives, who knows where it can lead? Maybe it will lead us to the more complex, critical, and risky places where we can make those decisions on a bigger and broader scale.

Maybe it will lead us to evaluate our situations differently. Maybe we'll come to believe that we can make a difference, that we can decide to be a neighbor to a complete stranger. Maybe we'll become stronger in our faith so that we can take some calculated risks for the sake of the gospel.

Maybe it will lead us to a better, stronger, more loving community and world.

Maybe it will lead us to the kingdom of God, right here on earth, if only for a moment.

Maybe... well, you never know.

Maybe... Amen.

Proper 11

Luke 10:38-42

Getters Of Things Done

Marys And Marthas

There are two kinds of people in the world: Marys and Marthas.

Marys are contemplative, cerebral, and serious-minded.

> They like to think about things. They want to see all of the angles, the different perspectives.
>
> They want to listen to both sides of the argument before they make up their mind.
>
> They are learners who love learning for its own sake.

Marthas are doers, workers, creators.

> They like to decide and act. They want to get going and get others going as well.
>
> They want to try things out and see what works and fix it as they go.
>
> They are getters of things done.

Marys love a good book and can spend a whole day reading and wonder where the time went.

Marthas love a job well done and can spend a whole day doing it but never have enough time.

Marys measure their love in words, in kind and gentle acts, gracefully given.

Marthas measure their love by the amount of callouses on their hands and the aches in their muscles.

Marthas are overachievers, probably the oldest children, responsible, hardworking, and parent pleasers.

They always know what to do.

Marys are sweet and thoughtful. Probably the youngest children, soft spoken, empathetic, and affectionate.

They always know what to say.

Marys think Marthas are crass and pushy, crude and rather vulgar the way they are always running here and there, never stopping to smell the flowers and enjoy life.

Marthas think Marys are slackers, lazy and worthless when there's work to be done, always sitting around thinking and reading and smelling flowers and never really accomplishing anything.

There are two kinds of people in the world: Marys and Marthas.

Which kind of person are you?

Are you a Mary or a Martha?

The Slacker And The Achiever

I don't know about you, but my first inclination upon reading or hearing read the story of Mary and Martha is to take sides. I'm betting it's the same for you.

Okay, be honest. Mary people, raise your hands. Martha people? Hands.

Uh, huh. Just as I thought.

In my experience, most people, when we're being honest, tend to see ourselves as Martha people — getters of things done. We see ourselves as workers hard at the task, pouring out our blood, sweat, toil, and tears for the good of all, right? Well, okay, maybe that's a little strong, but most of us tend toward the Martha side of the continuum, at least in our own eyes.

So, we're just a little bit taken aback when Jesus gently chastised Martha for getting on Mary's case. I mean, come on. She's up "to her eyeballs in soapsuds," as Fred Craddock put it, cooking, cleaning, serving, and refilling iced tea glasses. She was probably the one who ran the vacuum cleaner before the company arrived. Meanwhile, her sister was in the living room sitting at Jesus' feet, the place of a disciple, a *male* disciple, lapping up every word he said, no doubt batting her eyelashes and nodding like a bobblehead.

It's Martha who was fulfilling the cultural expectations for women of her time, doing what a good hostess does. Emily Post would be proud of her. Well — proud, that is, right up to the next moment when, frustrated and, no doubt, tired, she stormed into the living room, interrupted the conversation and, instead of addressing her sister, addressed Jesus.

"Master, Mary is not doing what a hostess is supposed to do. She's being a slacker. She's just sitting there on the floor, talking, when there's work to be done. What do you have to say about that?"

Jesus did, in fact, have something to say about that, but let's let that sit for a moment while we consider something else.

Let's leave Mary and Martha for a moment, bring down the lights on that side of the stage, and bring up the lights on the other side, stage right.

The Lawyer And The Rabbi

On that side of the stage, we have the story that we read last week.

Usually, this is referred to as the "Parable of the Good (or Helpful) Samaritan" and, certainly, it contained that story, that parable, but the good samaritan is really a story within a story. The main story started before the parable and ended after it. The real story, we could call the "Story of the Lawyer and the Rabbi".

You will recall, I think, that the samaritan parable was not told in a vacuum. It was, in fact, told in response to a question by a lawyer, a wordsmith who was testing Jesus' ability as a rabbi, also a wordsmith. "Who," the lawyer asked, "is my neighbor?"

Jesus answered with the parable, which we won't go over in detail, here. Just the bare bones: A man was traveling on a dangerous road where he was set upon by robbers who robbed him, beat him, and left him for dead beside the road.

Two good, upstanding, well and deservedly respected people

from the religious community came along and, for whatever reasons, they passed by without stopping. A third man, a member of a despised ethnic and religious minority, happened by and helped the man, doing more than even the most stringent moral code would require. End of parable.

Jesus then asked the lawyer, "Who was this man's neighbor?" And by "this man," he was talking about the victim. Who was the victim's neighbor?

The lawyer rightly said, "the one who helped him."

This is important because, if we aren't careful, we will flip-flop the roles. We will make the parable into a morality play; the lesson that anyone who is in need of help should be considered our neighbor.

But that is decidedly *not* the point that Jesus made with his question to the lawyer. Who, he wanted to know, was the wounded man's neighbor, and the answer was, the one who helped him.

In other words, you become a neighbor by helping someone who needs help.

And then, Jesus put a cap on the whole story, a cherry on the top of the sundae, an olive in the martini, with the last four words of the account, spoken to the lawyer: "Go and do likewise."

Did you hear that? "*Go and do*!"

That is the whole point of the story of the lawyer and the rabbi in which we find the story of the helpful samaritan. The most important word in the whole passage is *"do."*

Now, let's bring the lights back up stage left, where Mary, Martha, and Jesus were waiting.

Go And Do; Sit And Listen

What would Jesus say?

If he took Mary's side, she might never get up off the floor and Martha might just quit working and let the dishes pile up to the ceiling. Not a good outcome.

If he took Martha's side, the dishes would get done in a timely fashion, but important lessons would have been lost to the expediency of having a neat, clean kitchen.

So, what was he to do? What was he to say?

Before you answer, remember the lesson of the previous story, the story that commentators believe should always be told along with this one. The lesson of that story, you will recall, is *go and do.*

That lesson had already been delivered.

Now Jesus balanced the scales.

Martha, he said, "you are very busy doing lots of work, occupied by many things." (Okay, she's busy taking care of her guests, multitasking because she doesn't have any help. Nothing wrong with that, is there?)

But, Jesus said, there was one thing that was needed more than anything else, even more than the food and beverages you are serving to us and the dishes you are clearing and washing.

Whoa! These are fighting words to a Martha person. Are you telling me that what I'm doing isn't important? Hospitality was, after all, one of the most vital and important values in first-century Jewish culture. Hebrew scriptures are full of stories of how God rewarded people who showed hospitality and punished those who didn't.

Take another look at what happened to Sodom and Gomorrah if you doubt it.

In Genesis 24, Abraham's servant was so generously received by Rebekah at the well that he recognized her as the perfect wife for Isaac. And in the second book of Kings, the prophets Elijah and Elisha repaid their kind and generous hosts by curing their sons of life-threatening illnesses.

No, everything in Martha's background, everything in her life, everything she learned at her mother's knee and in Sunday school and Vacation Bible School taught her that hospitality wasn't just some optional thing you did from time to time. It was a moral imperative for the true people of God.

And hospitality was exactly the thing she was doing, here.

To make his point, Jesus used a food metaphor that was often missed by our translations.

Most translations have Jesus saying that, "Mary has chosen the better part." In fact, however, that word that is translated "part" can also be translated "portion." Mary has chosen the "better portion," as one might choose a better portion of meat or vegetables from a platter of food that was being offered.

Martha, who seemed to be obsessed with making sure everyone was fed and who would, as custom dictated, offer the best portions of the food to her guests, was now being told by Jesus that the better portions of food she was offering were not the most important thing.

There was a portion of food that was even better and more important than that which she had placed on the table and that was the food for the soul, that Jesus was offering through his words.

Martha, he seemed to be saying, the work of hospitality is all well and good because, through our generous treatment of others, we draw closer to YAWEH. But we can become so obsessed with our hospitality that it can actually become a distraction, a barrier between us and God.

When we work so hard at serving others, we may come to resent them...

When we work so long at being hospitable, we may grow angry at those we are called to welcome...

When we take the entire responsibility for hospitality upon our own shoulders, we may become aggrieved because others have not taken up the task with us...

When our devotion to the law is so obsessive, we may end up living our lives in a state of indignation, irritation, exasperation, and pique...

Before we come to any of those places, Jesus said, we must first learn to stop, to sit, to rest, to listen, and to learn from him.

Martha, lay down your scrub brush and towel. Sit. Listen.

Fred Craddock has placed these two stories — the story of the lawyer and the rabbi and the story of Mary and Martha in the same chapter of his commentary. They are always, he said, to be considered together.

And the lesson to be taken from them is this:

"There is a time to go and do; there is a time to listen and reflect.

Knowing which and when is a matter of spiritual discernment. If we were to ask Jesus which example applies to us, the Samaritan or Mary — his answer would probably be 'Yes.'"[10] Amen.

10 Fred B. Craddock, Interpretation: A Bible Commentary for Teaching and Preaching. Luke (Louisville: John Knox Press, 1990), 149-152.

Proper 12

Luke 11:1-13

A Sermon About Prayer

A responsible pastor must have a theology of prayer that goes beyond churchy axioms, pious clichés, pop theology, and Bible verses proof texted from the King James Bible.

An authentic theology of prayer must offer hope in the promise that God answers prayer, but it must also be prepared to respond to the questions of those whose prayers "availeth not." We must be, at once, ready to celebrate with those whose cancer went into remission and to weep with those whose cancer didn't, when both persons' prayers were equally frequent, fervent, and sincere. Our theology of prayer must address the disappointment of those who prayed passionately and endlessly that their child would recover from the injuries incurred in an automobile accident but watched their child die nonetheless. And it must address the joy of those who do not believe in prayer, who prayed not a word, and whose child recovered by what appeared to be a miracle.

In order to build such a theology of prayer, we turn to scripture, one passage of which is the gospel text for this Sunday. But we must be careful, for it is both informative and dangerous.

It can help us on our way to an informed, well-established theology of prayer. But it can also send us down all kinds of rabbit holes that lead to a prayerology that is ill informed, ill considered, unhelpful, sometimes hurtful, and often blasphemous.

So, we must consider it carefully.

To do so, I suggest we take the passage, verse by verse, examining each idea individually and then all of them together, as a whole.

> *1. He was praying in a certain place, and after he had finished, one of his disciples said to him, "Lord, teach us to pray, as John*

taught his disciples."

We start with the image of Jesus, himself, praying.

The subject of prayer is not an academic one for Jesus or for the author of this gospel.

The disciples approached Jesus while he was praying, not while he was writing a paper or a book about prayer. Prayer, Luke told us, is an activity that comes in the midst of life, a vital activity which should be approached not with academic detachment and objectivity, but with passion and a sense of urgency.

They did not ask him to teach them *about* prayer or to give them his theology of prayer. They asked him to teach them how to pray the way John taught his disciples.

Apparently, the disciples were impressed with the way John's disciples prayed. What it was about their prayers that was so impressive, we do not know. Were their prayers eloquent or poetic, lyrical, or beautifully worded? More likely, the prayers of John's disciples were passionate and fervent and it was this passion, this power that the disciples of Jesus wanted to emulate.

Jesus, however, offered them something different. No flailing about — no screaming and crying. No moaning, self-flagellation or weeping *mea culpa's.*

What Jesus offered them was prayer founded on and based in relationship.

> *2. He said to them, "When you pray, say: Father, hallowed be your name. Your kingdom come. 3. Give us each day our daily bread. 4. And forgive us our sins, for we ourselves forgive everyone indebted to us. And do not bring us to the time of trial."*

As protestants, many of us are averse to praying prescribed prayers, especially those written by other people in other times and places. We feel that, if we try to pray those prayers, God will think of us as un-spontaneous and, perhaps, insincere, as though we are plagiarizing another's work and claiming it as our own and God, like some cosmic college professor, will give us a failing grade in our prayer life.

Jesus seemed to have no problem with this notion, however,

he didn't say, "When you pray, pray something like this..." No, he said, "Whey you pray, say..." Say these words. *Pray this prayer.* Make it your own and use it.

The first word of the prayer showed that Jesus desired for us a closer, warmer, more intimate relationship with God. Not the relationship of penitent to priest, or claimant to judge. The relationship that Jesus wanted for us is one of child to parent.

When you come before God, come as a loving child to a loving parent, he said. And he said it with only one word: "Father." In fact, some scholars tell us that the proper translation of this word, "Abba" in the Aramaic, is something more like "daddy" than "father."

The name of God is so holy (hallowed) that we dare not say or even write it. Thus, do we acknowledge that God is God and we aren't. We come as supplicants, as creatures to the creator and we acknowledge that.

When we ask God to "Make your kingdom come," we are asking God to do what we know God is already doing. We are just saying that we are on board with that. It is what we want also. We want the justice, harmony, and joy that are promised to all people in God's kingdom and we want it, as God does, for all people.

We ask that God's will be done on earth as it is in heaven, that is, everywhere, all the time. Not just when it suits us or our purposes, but always.

Ask God to forgive your sins, Jesus said, not because you deserve to be forgiven, or because your sins weren't really all that bad, but because we know the value and the cost of forgiveness. We have demonstrated in our own lives that for which we ask.

And, finally, do not judge us. Some believe that this last line refers to the eschaton, the end of time, while others believe that it refers to the immediate now. I like to think that it refers to both. God, it said, please do not judge us now or in the future because, certainly, who among us can stand against your perfect judgment?

Having given us a perfect example of a prayer, Jesus taught a little bit about prayer.

5. And he said to them, "Suppose one of you has a friend, and you go to him at midnight and say to him, "Friend, lend me three loaves of bread; 6. for a friend of mine has arrived, and I have nothing to set before him.' 7. And he answers from within, "Do not bother me; the door has already been locked, and my children are with me in bed; I cannot get up and give you anything.' 8. I tell you, even though he will not get up and give him anything because he is his friend, at least because of his persistence he will get up and give him whatever he needs.

A curious parable, is it not? It is about a man with two friends and it is about the first-century semitic law and custom of hospitality.

Hospitality was, for first-century Jews, not a choice. One was expected to show hospitality to anyone who was in need of it, friends or strangers, but especially friends. Usually, this was done systemically by the village as a whole. Guest houses were provided for people traveling through the area who had no place to stay. Travelers might go to these places for food and shelter that was provided by everyone in the village, collectively.

Failing that, the village might allow sojourners to make their camp, for the night, around the well at the center of town and food would be provided for them by various townspeople.

Outside of towns and cities, in rural areas, first-century Jews were expected to invite travelers into their homes or camps and feed them, house them, and even protect them for a night. The torah required it.

"When an alien resides with you in your land, you shall not oppress the alien. The alien who resides with you shall be to you as the citizen among you; you shall love the alien as yourself, for you were aliens in the land of Egypt..." (Leviticus 19:33-34).

If the law applied that strictly to gentiles and foreigners, how much more must it have applied to fellow Jews? And more still to Jewish friends?

Here, in the story, we have a man, who was a Jew, who was visited, unexpectedly, by a Jewish friend. Certainly, the story did not suggest that the man's larder was completely empty but that it contained nothing of sufficient quality to lay before a hungry friend. So, he went next door to his other friend and asked for help.

But this friend, even knowing what was at stake, refused to help and his only excuse was that he was too lazy to help. That his kids were asleep and he might wake them up can surely not be convincing given all of the pounding and hollering that is going on in this house at midnight. But he was, as some scholars insisted, shameless. Even though he would be judged just as harshly for leaving a traveler stranded and hungry, he didn't care. He couldn't be bothered.

Except the desperate friend and host did not let him off so easily. He kept on knocking and pounding on the door, begging for help and so the man got out of bed and gave the man what he needed, not because they were friends, not because there was a hungry stranger who needed help, but because of the friends' incessant knocking and calling out to him.

Was Jesus saying that we can badger and cajole God into giving us what we want? Was he saying that God was like a curmudgeonly old man who doesn't want to get off the couch but would relent just to get us off his back?

No, of course not.

What Jesus was saying, I believe, was that, if a friend, who should be willing and even eager to help you must be cajoled into it through constant badgering, then how much more would God be willing to help - God, who is loving, kind, generous, and anxious to help his needful children?

Hence the next two verses:

> *9. "So I say to you, Ask, and it will be given you; search, and you will find; knock, and the door will be opened for you. 10. For everyone who asks receives, and everyone who searches finds, and for everyone who knocks, the door will be opened.*

Be careful.

This is a dangerous passage that we dare not toss off the cuff without giving it some serious thought. Because, let us be honest, there are more than a few people — sitting in our pews, living in the houses in our neighborhoods, occupying the desks in our classrooms, driving in our carpools, and sitting in the break room across the table from us — who have searched diligently without finding, knocked until their knuckles were bloody and still faced a closed door, asked without receiving, and searched without finding.

People we know and love have left the church because their prayers did not lift their despair, heal their broken hearts, mend their husband's injured spine, or make life even one iota easier for their disabled child.

And, that being the case, they were left with only one of two conclusions: a) either the passage is at best a naïve error or, at worst, a deliberate lie, or b) that the verse is true and the disappointment is their own fault because they didn't search in the right places, knock on the right doors, or ask the right questions. Or, if they did do all these things, they did not do them with enough passion or faith.

I do not think that is so, nor do I believe it wise to tell someone that this passage promises that God will give us whatever we ask for if we ask for it in the appropriate way with the appropriate measure of faith and sincerity.

I do not believe that God sits upon a judgment throne, listening to our prayers and saying, things like, "Oh, Janet, I would have loved to cure your child's spina bifida, and I would have, if only you would have used the right words in your petition." I do not believe that God hears a prayer and says, "Oh, Bill, I would have loved to deliver your son from his addiction and I would have if only you'd had five or six more people praying for him." Or, "Oh, Mary Margaret, I would have loved to give you an A on that test and I would have, but your prayer lacked sufficient urgency for that kind of miracle."

I do not know why some people get what they pray for and others don't. I do not know why some people get things, good things, that they haven't prayed for and others, good people, who have prayed for those very things do not receive them.

I do not know these things and I would not dare to try to

come up with some explanation that would be little more than ill-informed guesswork.

But I do believe this:

The God who comes to us in the person of Jesus Christ, is a loving, caring God who has numbered the hairs on our heads, who searches for us when we are lost, who weeps with us when we are in pain, and who dances with us when we are enraptured with joy.

And I believe that that God wants only good things for us. How do I know? The Bible tells me so. Listen:

"Is there anyone among you who, if your child asks for a fish, will give a snake instead of a fish? Or if the child asks for an egg, will give a scorpion? If you then, who are evil, know how to give good gifts to your children, how much more will the heavenly Father give the Holy Spirit to those who ask him!"(11:11-13)

Luke set us up with what is called a parallelism.

First example of the parallelism:

If your child, whom you love, asks for a fish, would you give him a snake?

No, of course not.

Second example of the parallelism:

If your child, whom you love, asks for an egg, would you give her a scorpion?

Again, no, of course not.

Third example of the parallelism:

Nope, Luke breaks the parallelism to give his point greater emphasis.

So, if you, who are sinful want only good things for your children, then how much more does God, who is good, want good things for you? So that, if you ask for the Holy Spirit, he will, of course, give it to you.

The disciples began this passage asking Jesus to teach them how to pray but Jesus answered by giving them a lesson on how to have an appropriate relationship with God, a relationship that is like that of a loving, admiring, child to a kind and loving parent.

The appropriate prayer is the prayer that begins with the

knowledge that we are the creature and God is the Creator, we are needy and God is generous, we are powerless and God is omnipotent, we are children and God is Abba.

And, when all is said and done, we stand with Job, acknowledging that we do not have the answers to all of our questions about prayer. We can't explain all the things that we do not understand about it and we do not even have the words with which to ask.

What we do have is this:

We have faith that God loves us and walks with us through even the darkest night.

We have the Holy Spirit, whom God has given to us to accompany us when we feel alone, to warm us when we feel cold, and to prop us up when we feel weak.

These we have, not because we deserve them, but because we have come, in faith, to a loving, generous God. Amen.

Proper 13

Luke 12:13-21

The Mother Of All Yard Sales

> And he said to them, "Take care! Be on your guard against all kinds of greed; for one's life does not consist in the abundance of possessions."
>
> Luke 12:15

Three years ago, I retired from the active ministry and moved into a new phase of my career. I still preach, write, and teach, from time to time. I just am not *required* to do that.

Besides moving into a new kind of ministry, my wife and I also moved into a new house. New for us, at any rate.

Once we bought the house and set the closing and moving dates, it became clear that the house we were moving into was not nearly big enough to hold all the stuff we were going to be moving out of the church parsonage.

We were moving from a 2,500 square foot, ten-room house into a 1,500 square foot, six-room house. So, we sat down and talked, then decided that this move would necessitate our getting rid of about 2/3 of everything we owned.

Jean was remarkably agreeable to this with only one demand: *no yard sale.*

I quickly acquiesced to that demand as there was a very good and sound reason for it.

Sixteen years previously, we had moved from Columbus, Ohio, to Wilmington, Ohio, under much the same circumstances. The house we were moving from was roughly the same size as the house we were moving to, except that the house we were moving from had a basement and the one we were going to did not.

We had lived in that house for eleven years and it's amazing how much stuff you can accumulate, especially in a basement, over eleven years.

Also, both of our kids who had been commuting to college from home were now going to be moving onto the college campus.

There was, to put it simply, lots of stuff to get rid of.

We decided to have a yard sale. Not just any yard sale, mind you. This, our kids proudly announced, would be the *mother of all yard sales*! It would be a yard sale that would demand an unfailing ruthlessness from us as we sorted what would be kept and what would be sold, what we really needed and what we could live without.

I'm not embarrassed to say that I took the lead in this effort. I was relentless in my pursuit and identification of unnecessary stuff. Tears did not deter me. Pleading did not deter me. Begging only hardened my resolve. My family would, I was determined, learn to live with less. It was not an easy task but a necessary one and one to which I was more than equal.

I whittled, pared, slashed, cut, and, finally, I managed to reduce the belongings of my wife and children to manageable and reasonable quantities. Everything else went into the yard sale.

Then, to demonstrate my fair-mindedness, I allowed them to examine my things and hold forth on what of mine would be saved and what would go into the sale.

Some of you have met my wife and children.

Let me warn you that even though they seem to be nice, polite, sensitive people, that appearance is nothing more than an elaborate and clever façade.

Never have I seen such vicious and spiteful behavior. I witnessed a whole new side of my family that I had never seen before — a grossly insensitive and (dare I say) mean side. Yes, when it comes to other people's property, my family knows not even a drop of the milk of human kindness.

They had the temerity to suggest that I did not actually need all four of the rubber chickens that graced my study — gifts lovingly given to me by various youth groups that I had faithfully led through the years. They had the brutal insensitivity to insist that just because I never cook in a cast-iron skillet, I should live with only one of the six that I had saved. Never mind that my grandmother and my mother had given me two of those skillets; I just couldn't remember which ones. They even launched personal attacks on my self-control and discipline, implying with winks and nods that I was never going to lose enough weight to get into all those clothes that I had saved — blue jeans and t-shirts that were in perfectly good condition except for the shrinkage which would require me to return to those svelte days of yesteryear, which I certainly intended to do.

No amount of reason could dissuade them. No flood of impassioned oratory would divert them. No avalanche of pouting, whining, pleading, and begging would turn them from their course. They had hardened their hearts against me. Some of my most valuable things went into the yard sale.

Then, as if to add insult to injury, they priced those valued possessions miles below what they were worth. I could not but weep as I watched my classic Levis 501 button-fly jeans sell for a mere dollar a pair. I writhed in agony as my beloved skillets sold for fifty cents each, all five for two dollars. I winced as my rubber chickens were carted off for a mere 25 cents apiece.

It was a brutal, painful, dismal affair, that *mother-of-all-yard-sales*. It was painful for all concerned except maybe the guy who bought the rubber chickens. He seemed to be having a great time. But for my family, it was a disaster, emotionally if not financially.

In one, brief, Saturday morning and afternoon, we were confronted (frankly and painfully) with just how connected, how attached, how cemented we are to the stuff of this world. We are a Christian family and we desire and try daily to follow the teachings of our Lord Jesus Christ. But nowhere is there a more difficult teaching than the one he has given to us about our appropriate relationship to "things." And we struggle with it daily.

You Are What You Own

And why shouldn't we? We live in a culture which constantly bombards us with the message that you are what you own.

Do you want to be smart? Buy this. Do you want to be pretty? Buy that. Do you want to be successful? Acquire this. Do you want to be admired and desired? Own that.

I recently heard, on a radio program, that within hours of the end of the Tour de France bicycle race, people were going into bike shops asking to buy the very same bicycle that the winner had ridden.

The bike shop owner said that, while he was glad for the business, he had to be honest with his potential customers and tell them that, first of all, they couldn't afford the bicycle that the winner of the tour was riding. It was a highly specialized, custom, hand-built set of bicycles paid for by corporate sponsors. And secondly, even if they could get a bicycle like that, they could not even begin to do with it what the winner of the tour did. His accomplishment was not just about his bicycle. It was more about his genetics, his determination, his discipline, and his monomaniacal obsession with that one race.

Try as he could, however, that admirably honest merchant was most often unable to dissuade his customers from buying the most expensive bicycle they could find, convinced that it would improve their performance in ways that they could not do with self-discipline and hard training.

I'm a golfer and we are a gadget loving bunch, almost as bad as those who fish for the wily and elusive largemouth bass.

Several years ago, a craze hit the golfing world in the shape of a golf ball called the Lady Precept. Word got around that some of the pro golfers on the Seniors (now Champions) tour, were using a pink ball that was made, specifically for women golfers: The Lady Precept. Word had it that those guys were adding ten to twenty yards to their drives by using that ball.

Suddenly, you couldn't buy that ball for love or money. Everyone had to have it. In some cases, the stories went, guys who were embarrassed to buy a ball made for women golfers, were sending their wives into the pro shops to buy them.

A teaching pro explained the irony of this obsession with a pink golf ball:

The Lady Precept was designed for women because women tend to swing the club slower than men, which means they aren't hitting the ball as hard. The ball works as designed, he explained, only if you swing the club slowly. But men, being men, couldn't bring themselves to slow their swing. They would tee up their little pink Lady Precept and then flail away just like they always did, and the new ball would do what their old golf balls always did.

"Then they came in here mad at me," he went on, "because the ball wasn't doing what they thought it would do."

I was at a golf show one time where businesses were touting the latest technologies and equipment and trying to get us to buy it when I came upon a booth where a guy was selling little glassine bags full of golf tees. He swore that the special, goofy looking design of this particular tee would increase your drive by three to five yards. He was selling them faster than he could ring them up.

I remember a conversation I had with my Uncle Waldo, my dad's brother, when I was a little boy. Waldo was an avid fisherman with a tackle box big enough to park your car in, or so it seemed to me. He and I were fishing in a boat on a lake one day and I was looking through his tackle box at all of the dozens of fishing lures he had in there.

I pointed to a huge one, maybe four or five inches long. "Waldo, what is this one called?"

"That's a Lazy Ike," he said.

"What do you catch with it?" I asked.

"Nothing, so far," he said.

"Then why did you buy it?"

"I thought it might catch something. The guy at the store told me it would catch Northern Pike."

"But it didn't catch Northern Pike?"

"Nope. Not for me it didn't."

"Are you sad that you bought it?"

He looked, twitched his rod a little, then looked down at his tackle box. "Dean, to tell you the truth, I haven't caught fish on most of the lures in that box. But you don't know until you try them and, I can't help myself. I see a lure; I just have to try it."

Golfers, fishermen, bowlers, writers, even television watchers — we are all convinced that no matter how good we are or how much enjoyment we are getting from the activity in which we are engaged, there is something out there that, if we could only afford to buy it, would vastly increase the level of our ability and depth of our pleasure.

A Matter Of Authenticity

Now, no one would be so foolish as to suggest that "things" aren't important at all. Certainly, you will never hear me say that. I own the best golf clubs I can reasonably afford. I have a Kindle that I really like and two computers — one for on my desk and one for on the go. I like having cable and Jean and I constantly remind each other how much we love our home, small as it is.

We all like things. Things are important.

Things have the ability to make our lives simpler, easier, quicker, and more enjoyable. They can make us more productive, more creative, more clever, and more knowledgeable. But there is one thing that things can't do. They can't make us more authentic.

They can't make our lives more authentically human.

Only God can do that.

In the gospel lesson for today, a man came to Jesus and asked him to intervene on his behalf. The man was obviously the younger of two brothers and, according to ancient Jewish and mid-eastern custom, the family inheritance went totally to the firstborn son. The older brother would become the head of the family and the younger brother would probably become an employee of the family estate.

The young man saw this as unfair. Why should the older brother receive the wealth and the status of the family inheritance simply because he was born earlier? What had he done to deserve it? How had he earned it? It was not fair! The only fair thing would be for the inheritance to be divided equally between the two brothers.

The father, however, had spent his entire life building up the estate that he probably inherited from his father. It represented security and status for his heirs long after he was dead and gone. He was not about to see it broken apart and divided. He wanted to see it kept intact. So, he left it to the oldest son, according to the custom.

Jesus saw that the real issue here was not about the relative fairness or unfairness of the traditional Jewish inheritance customs. It was about a man that saw his life as worthless, inauthentic, and not worth living unless it was accompanied by a vast quantity of things and all that those things represented.

He responded to the man with a parable of another man who had many things and wanted even more. Notice that there was, in the story, no condemnation of wanting things and working hard to get them. The error of the man in the parable was not in having things, but in his relationship to those things. He was not a fool for working hard. He was not a fool for building up a large savings account. He was not a fool for putting something back for a rainy day.

He was a fool because he thought those things would make his life secure. He was a fool because he thought that his life was controlled by what he owned. He was a fool because he had confused who he was with what he had. He was a fool because he had confused the well-supplied life with the well-lived life and the contents of his wallet with the contents of his heart and his character.

The authentic life, said Jesus over and over again, throughout the gospels, was the life lived in the midst of things but not enslaved to them. It is the life lived by those who own their possessions and are not owned by them. It is the life lived by the one who knows that only to the degree that we are detached from what we own can we be attached to God as God comes to us in Jesus Christ.

The authentic life is the life lived by one who knows that sometimes we have to have the *mother of all yard sales* if we want to take our seat beside the Father of all creation. Amen.

Proper 14

Luke: 12:32-40

The Main Thing

> For where your treasure is, there your heart will be also. Luke 12:34
>
> "The main thing is to keep the main thing the main thing."[11]

The main thing is to keep the main thing the main thing.

That's important. You might want to write it down.

I'll say it again: The main thing is to keep the main thing the main thing. It's one of those seemingly self-evident rules that is absolutely essential if you want to succeed at anything. My Uncle John had a colorful way of illustrating the essential truth of it.

Uncle John, my mother's youngest brother, was sort of the bad egg of our family, the prodigal, the miscreant, and a man about whom will you probably hear many stories in my sermons. He was an alcoholic and a roustabout. He bragged that his poor choices had never landed him in prison and he had only done what he called "short time" in a few jails.

He would show up at our house about every four or five years when I was growing up and he would be broke and out of work, his belongings in a cardboard box or a shopping bag and his pickup truck barely running, if he even had a truck. Sometimes he called from the bus depot.

My parents would take him in and help him get back on his feet and then he would find some pretext for becoming offended and storming out only to show up again four or five years later in exactly the same state. One of the reasons for my Uncle John's

11 Stephen R. Covey, *7 Habits of Highly Effective People (London: Mango Media, 1989).*

lack of success in his life, besides the alcohol and the bad choices, was a complete inability to focus.

I talked to him about it one time and he explained to me how life seemed to always work for him:

> *"I was fixin' to eat a cheese sandwich, see. Just a plain ol' cheese sandwich, slice of Swiss cheese on bread with a little mustard. Well, don't you know that slice o' cheese had this piece of plastic stuck to it. So, I peel the plastic off and I take it to throw it in the trash. Only the trash can is filled up to where it's piled up against the wall. So, I go get a garbage bag to put the trash in and I take it out to the garbage can and wouldn't you know a dog or a coon or something has got into the garbage can and turned it over, spilling garbage all over. So, I go to the tool shed to get a shovel and rake to clean up the mess and I see there's a huge, I'm talking gigantic hornets' nest up in the corner near the door. Well, if I don't do something about those hornets, someone's gonna get stung cause that's how hornets are; they'll sting you just to see the look on your face. So, I get into the truck to go over to the hardware to get some hornet spray but the battery's dead on account of I left the dome light on the night before. So I go over to Carl's yonder to see if he can jump my truck but he's up on the roof of his house, replacing some shingles that blew off in that storm two weeks ago and he says he can't come down until he gets that hole in his roof patched or Mary Ann'll skin him, but he'll help me start my truck as soon as he gets the job done.*
>
> *"So that's how I end up on my neighbor's roof, nailing down shingles when all I really wanted to do was eat a cheese sandwich."*

We've all probably had an experience like that, if not quite that extreme. John's problem was that his entire life was like that. He just couldn't seem to keep the main thing the main thing.

In any human endeavor, if we want to succeed, we must be able to focus. Whether reroofing our house, eating a cheese sandwich, or something vastly more important than either of those, like being an authentic Christian person. Focus is an essential ingredient in any kind of success.

The task which lies before us as Christians, is considerably more difficult, complex, and important than eating a cheese sandwich, yet distraction is just as big a problem in the spiritual aspect of life as it is in any other part. Even as we pursue the most important task of our lives — following Jesus — distractions arise.

The author and the historic editors of the gospel of Luke understood this dilemma. They have taken two separate stories or parables used by Jesus to demonstrate and warn us against the problem of distractions and put them together in the gospel lesson for this morning.

One is the parable of the watchmen waiting for the master of the house. The other is the story of the man whose house was burglarized. In both stories we see the importance of being awake, alert, and aware, focused on the task at hand. In the first story, those who were focused were rewarded. In the second, those who were unfocused suffered painful loss. As is always the case with parables, the characters and the events which inhabit them are metaphors for life in and out of the kingdom of God.

To understand the message of the parables, we have to unpack their symbolism so that it can speak to our lives and times. Clearly the stories are speaking to us about the appropriate life of the faithful, authentic Christian. And both of the stories tell us that the faithful, authentic Christian life is one of focused watchfulness. The watchmen are watchful for the return of their master, the wedding guest. The homeowner should have been watchful for those who would break into and burglarize his home. The question before us, as Christians, is this: For what should we be watchful? What is it that we are looking for? What is it that we are waiting for? Upon what should we be focused?

To put it in modern vernacular — What is the main thing of Christian living?

The Main Thing

The main thing of Christian living is no different today than it was two thousand years ago. Two thousand years ago, the main thing of those early Jewish Christians was no different than it was for their forefathers and foremothers a thousand years before that.

We find it written in the book of Deuteronomy, Chapter 6, verse 4 and following. In Hebrew it is called the Shema, and when Jesus was asked which commandment was the greatest, he recited it to his listeners. (Matt 22: 37ff; Luke 10:27ff; Mark 12: 29ff)

Hear, O Israel! The Lord is our God, the Lord is one!

And you shall love the Lord your God with all your heart and with all your soul and with all your might.

The task of every Christian, the main thing, if you will, is to have a personal, loving, faithful relationship with God. That was the task which challenged Abraham and compelled Moses. It was the task that empowered Joseph and frustrated David. It was that task that inspired courage in Esther and faith in Ruth, which enflamed the Maccabees, comforted Mary, impassioned John the Baptist, consumed Jesus, and drove Paul. It is that task which stands before the contemporary people of God no less now than it stood before every person of God over the past four millennia. Indeed, it is that task which stands before us this day and will stand before us tomorrow as we rise for work and school and play. As Christians, we qualify the task by adding only one phrase.

To have and maintain a personal loving, faithful relationship with God ***as he comes to us in Jesus Christ.***

But how do we do that? What activities do we pursue? What books do we read? What rituals do we perform? What phrases do we recite? How does one have and maintain a personal, loving, faithful relationship with God? Well, scripture and experience tell us that we have a personal, loving, faithful relationship with God the same way we have a personal, loving, faithful relationship with anyone.

First, we commit ourselves to having that relationship. That is, we make a commitment; we decide to be in the relationship.

One of the things I point out to a couple who come to me

to be married is that when they take their vow to love, cherish, honor, and keep their spouse, they do not say "I do." They say, "I will." That is, they make a decision and a commitment to be in the relationship regardless of what may come. When they say, "I will," they are saying that they will love and cherish, honor, and take care of this person regardless of how they may feel on any given day or at any given moment. Come fat or bald, come sickness or health, come rich or poor, they will pursue and maintain this relationship. Love, in this instance, is first and foremost, a decision.

If we want to have and maintain a personal, loving, faithful relationship, the first thing we do is to decide and commit.

The second thing we do is be attentive. That is, we watch.

No relationship is successful because we committed to it once and then put it in the back of our minds. A relationship that succeeds over time in being personal, loving, and faithful, is one that is attended to and fed regularly. This is true of marriage relationships, working relationships, parental relationships, and friendships.

My wife and I will celebrate our fiftieth wedding anniversary in July of 2022 and I can tell you with some considerable confidence that no marriage lasts fifty years. It lasts for 18,250 days. (That's the number of days in fifty years.)

It lasts because every morning for 18,250 days, two people decide to be married to each other, and let's face it, no one wants to be married to that same person every day for 18,250 days.

Sometimes I wake up wondering, "What was I thinking?" And sometimes so does she.

But it doesn't really matter because we made a commitment and we decided then and we decide every, single morning that we're going to be married, today. And tomorrow - and the day and the days after that, until we die. Every time we have a chance, we renew that commitment, not in front of the church but in front of each other.

We laugh together, we cry together, we kiss, we hug, we ask each other's opinion, we share our ideas and feelings, we hold hands, and, sometimes we still manage to surprise each other.

If we want to have and maintain a personal, loving faithful relationship, the first thing we do is to decide to commit to the relationship. The second thing we do is realize that the decision is one that is made not once, but ten thousand times; the commitment is renewed every day, and sometimes every hour, whenever the opportunity presents itself.

If these things are true in human relationships, how much more true are they in our relationship with God? If we want to have a close, personal, loving, faithful relationship with God, we must commit to the relationship and attend to the maintenance of it every time an opportunity comes along. The trick is to be constantly watching so we recognize those opportunities when they present themselves because they often appear when and from where we least expect it.

Distractions

The witness of scripture and history, as well as our own experience tells us that the opportunity to renew our relationship with God can come from any direction at any time.

The prophet Isaiah first heard the call and demand of God on his life while he stood in the temple during the funeral service of King Uzziah. He found his relationship with God renewed when he brought God's word to the people.

Jeremiah came to know God in a dream that he had as a teenager and renewed his relationship with God through his own suffering and his work on behalf of the poor and the oppressed.

Moses went to the mountaintop, David went to music and poetry, Gideon went into battle, and Paul was going to Damascus. Their encounters with God were as different as they were authentic and compelling.

John Wesley met God in a Bible study with people from another Christian denomination from his own. Harry Emerson Fosdick came to a personal knowledge of God's grace as he recovered from what, today, we might call a nervous breakdown, and Mother Teresa said she saw God in the eyes of the sick and the poor to whom she ministered on the streets of Calcutta.

The undeniable fact that comes to us in the lives of the saints is that God comes to us in a thousand different ways from a thousand different directions and it is up to us to be ready to discern God's presence in our lives.

But distractions abound, don't they?

We get distracted by fatigue.

The watchmen in the parable stand through the night near the gate and with each passing hour, the work of the day takes a heavier toll. Their eyelids become heavy and their senses dull. They want to rest more than they want to watch.

We work hard all week, on the job and at home, and when Sunday morning comes, our eyes grow heavy with the fatigue that has built in us all week and we want to trade that hour at church for just one more precious hour of sleep.

We get distracted by doubt.

The watchmen in the parable stood at the gate and waited for the master's return. They didn't expect him to return immediately, so they didn't worry about it for the first few hours. But then, after a few hours, in what is called the second watch, they began to note that it was getting late and he should have been back by then. By the third watch they had given up, convinced that he wasn't coming. They just didn't believe anymore.

And so it is with us. We have convinced ourselves that God always comes in a certain way at a certain hour and, when God fails to show as we expect, we give up.

We get distracted by false messiahs.

Spend a few moments browsing through the self-help section of the books on Amazon and it doesn't take long to see that there are messiahs everywhere. They all have a path, a plan, a prayer, a gimmick, a gizmo, a formula, or a fad that is going to save your life or your marriage, make you richer or thinner - or both.

Our culture is a veritable breeding ground for false messiahs. The path to a truly authentic life, we are told, can be purchased for just three easy payments of $19.95 plus shipping and handling.

The prophet, Isaiah, pointed out that even our religion can be an idol if we approach it without faith. Listen to what he has to say to the devoutly religious people of his time who have put more effort into their rituals and practices than into their moral lives:

I have had enough of burnt offerings of rams, and the fat of fed cattle.

I take no pleasure in the blood of bulls, lambs, or goats.

Bring your worthless offerings no longer,

Their smell is an abomination to me.

I hate your new moon festivals and your appointed feasts.

They have become a burden to me and I am weary of bearing them.

The people to whom Isaiah was talking had become more interested in the smells and bells of their religion than they were in living and loving it. They had turned away from the business of faith in favor of the busy-ness of religion.

Their religion had become a false messiah, and false messiahs are the greatest enemies of the watchfulness that God requires of us. They distract us from our relationships with God and each other.

Wake-Up Call

The parables that Luke gave us in today's gospel text are, literally, wake-up calls. He invited us to ask ourselves the crucial question of the Christian life: Have we kept the main thing the main thing? Or have we fallen asleep?

Have we drifted into slumber, victims of the fatigue that our lifestyle places upon us?

Have we allowed ourselves to be lulled into unbelief because God didn't do what we expected or wanted and when we expected or wanted it done?

Have we been seduced by false messiahs? Have we been distracted by the promises of the flashy and the attractive, the entertaining and the instantaneous?

If, indeed, we find ourselves saying yes to any of these questions, then Jesus, speaking through the gospel writer Luke, says this:

Wake up!

Stay awake! Keep watching!

The kingdom of God is coming to you when and where you least expect it.

Is it in the person sitting in front of you or behind you in church?

Is it in the person you will greet as you leave the sanctuary? Or maybe it won't be in the church at all. Maybe it will be at work, at school, at the PTA meeting, the bowling alley, or at the mall.

But, of this you can be sure. This we can take to the bank. This we can stake our life upon.

It will be!

Behold, the kingdom of God is at hand. It is God's gift to us.

Watch for it!

It is, after all, the main thing. Amen.

Proper 15

Luke 12:49-56

Good News / Bad News

> Do you think I came to bring peace on earth? No, I tell you, but division. Luke 12:51

Sports writers still talk about the joy they used to take in interviewing the great New York Yankees catcher, Yogi Berra. Yogi was something of a rough-hewn philosopher given to malaprops and seemingly contradictory statements that managed to, somehow, still make a weird kind of sense.

It was Yogi who said: "It ain't over 'til it's over." And, "It's like déjà vu all over again." When giving his opinion of a New York restaurant, he's reported to have said, "Nobody goes there anymore; it's too crowded." And, he may be best known for his advice to young people: "When you come to a fork in the road, take it."

When you come to a fork in the road, take it.

One of the things that made Yogi's aphorisms so funny and memorable was that even though they seemed paradoxical or hyper-obvious, there was, hidden within them, a little bit of wisdom. When you come to a fork in the road, take it. Life is nothing if not a series of forks in the road, decisions waiting to be made. And often, the consequences of those decisions will have effects more far-reaching and determinative than we ever imagined at the decisive moment.

What might my life have looked like had I not decided to swallow my anxiety and call Jean Herzog for a date 48 years ago? Which direction might my life have taken if, for our first date, I had decided to take her to a movie instead of trick-or-treating for UNICEF with the children of our church? How might my life have gone had I not, one day, apropos to nothing, asked my dad to teach me how to read music? And where might I have ended up, had I blown off that meeting at our church where the dean of the seminary was speaking?

Each one of these was a choice I made, a small choice in the grand scheme of things, but a choice that ended up affecting the direction of my entire life. And each one is a choice I'm glad I made.

Christianity is another choice I made. And usually, I'm glad I made it — usually.

But, you know, it's not always easy being a Christian.

Jesus understood that his way was not always the easiest way to follow. Later, when the writers and editors of the gospels wrote down their versions of Jesus' life, the list of Christian martyrs was already a long one. Peter and Paul had died with some 2,000 other Christians in Nero's purges. Stephen had been stoned to death and James had been thrown from the pinnacle of the temple and then beaten to death when the fall didn't kill him. Those early chroniclers of Christianity had come to realize that Christianity, or what they called, "The Way" was a road that was rarely easy to follow and often littered with obstacles, trials, pitfalls, difficulties, and, sometimes, bodies.

That reality is made fully if painfully clear in the gospel lesson for today and, if we want to be serious about our lives as Christians, we would do well to look carefully at this difficult passage and heed it as we renew daily our decision for Christ.

The first three verses make that point clearly:

> *I came to bring fire to the earth and how I wish it were already kindled!* (Luke 12:49).

My good friend, Max, once sat on a taskforce which our bishop created, the purpose of which was to help re-invigorate, refresh, and renew the ministry that was taking place in the churches of our conference. Shortly after the first meeting of the taskforce, I met Max for one of our bi-monthly lunches and asked him how things went at the meeting. I asked what his impression was of the new bishop.

He laid his sandwich down and leaned back in his chair, wiped his mouth with his napkin, and said, "Well, Dean, there's good news and bad news. The good news is that this new bishop wants to breathe a breath of fresh air into the conference. He's going to encourage evangelism, good preaching, missional outreach, and he's going to cut out some of the deadwood that has been putting a drag on our districts and clogging the pulpits of Ohio for the last twelve years."

That all sounded great to me. "What's the bad news?" I asked him.

He leaned forward conspiratorially, looked around, and said, "I think I'm the deadwood... and I'm not sure about you."

We had a good laugh. Of course, we don't ever think of ourselves as deadwood... but you never know.

Jesus' pronouncement that he had come to bring fire to the earth was an example of good news and bad news. This is hardly the "gentle Jesus, meek and mild" that we have come to love and expect from our Sunday School songs. This is not the soft spoken, mild mannered, inoffensive Jesus of the old paintings and movies of our youth. This is a Jesus who has good news and bad news and he delivers it in the form of a metaphor: fire.

To the ancient near-eastern listeners for whom these words were first spoken, fire was both a gift and a curse. It was a wonderful tool to be used with caution because it had terrible destructive potential. Fire warmed the home, lighted the darkness, and purified that which was contaminated. But it also had the potential to destroy the very house that it warmed and inflict terrible pain and suffering on those to whom it gave comfort.

The gospel writer, Luke, understood that delicate balance that fire represented in the symbolic life of the church. The gospel, the good news of Jesus Christ, the real presence of God's kingdom in this life, was like fire, he said. It has the power to light the darkness in our lives. It has the power to warm our hearts when they are cold and to purify our lives when they are contaminated and soiled with sin and estrangement.

But there is another side to the gospel, a side about which we do not often hear or speak, a side which can cause pain, tears, and division even within families.

> *I have a baptism with which to be baptized, and what stress I am under until it is completed!* (Luke 12:50).

For years, when scholars read this verse about the baptism that Jesus was yet to experience and the anticipation of which was placing so much stress on his life, they assumed that he was talking about his crucifixion. But I have come to believe with more recent scholarship that the baptism metaphor represents a broader and more inclusive kind of conflict, one which culminated with his death but included other kinds of conflict and opposition.

The word, "completed," can also be translated as "concluded" meaning that Jesus was talking about not one event but a series of events or a process that would unfold in stages — the opposition of the Pharisees, the contempt of the priests, the rejection by those in his own home town, the arrest by the priests, the betrayal of Judas, Peter, and even his closest friends, the scourging, the suffering, and, finally the crucifixion.

Jesus understood that The Way was not going to be easy for him and neither is it going to be easy for those who choose to follow him in it. Later he would speak of his road as one upon which you must "take up your cross."

Finally, in verse 51 he laid it all out for even the most clueless listener.

> *Do you think that I have come to bring peace to earth? No, I tell you, but rather division!*

And then he followed up this general statement with several examples of the kind of division and conflict that the gospel can cause. Groups of friends can be divided against each other; even families can find themselves in conflict over the demands of the gospel.

My friend and golf buddy, Darren, told of an occasion when one of the teens in his church who had gone off to college, came home for a visit at Christmas time. Ron dropped by the church to say hello and chat with Darren, his pastor, and eventually the conversation rolled around to the topic that was really on Ron's mind. He needed Darren's help.

"I've decided that I'm being called to the ministry," Ron said.

Darren was delighted to hear the news. Ron had been an active member in the youth fellowship for all of his middle school and high school career. His values and interests as well as his gifts and graces seemed to be well suited for the professional ministry. Darren was also a little flattered that Ron had come to him with this decision and was all ready to explain the process by which the United Methodist Church brought its ministers to ordination. He was also ready to recommend a couple of good seminaries when Ron stopped him. That stuff would come sometime down the road, he said. Right now, however, he needed a different kind of help.

"Sure," Darren said. "Name it."

Ron swallowed and took a deep breath. "I need you to come with me and be there when I tell my parents. This is going to kill them."

Darren said that it hit him like a blast of cold air when he realized the truth of what Ron was saying. Ron's dad was a firefighter. His uncle, his dad's brother, was a firefighter. His grandfather, his dad's father, was a firefighter. Ron's parents had just assumed that their oldest son would grow up to be a firefighter. They had groomed him for it. They had prepared him for it. They had indoctrinated him into it. His bedroom at home was decorated with firefighter paraphernalia. College was, for them, just something to do until he was old enough to apply to the city fire department. Ron was right. If this announcement didn't kill them, it would certainly blow a wide hole in their expectations for their son.

Darren went with him to break the news and, he said, there were some minor fireworks — some tears — some remonstrations and recriminations. On the other hand, having the minister go with you to tell your parents you want to be a minister isn't a bad idea. How many bad things could they say about the ministry with their minister sitting right there?

Today, Ron is a pastor and his parents have come around,

somewhat. Darren reported that, while they are cordial, they are also a bit distant with him. Word has it that they harbor some resentment that their son came to him before he came to them and they felt the pastor should have worked harder to talk some sense into their son.

Decision And Division

"Although the kingdom of God is (usually) characterized by reconciliation and peace," said New Testament scholar Alan Culpepper, "the announcement of that kingdom is always divisive because it requires decision and commitment" (*New Interpreter's Bible,* Vol IX, p. 266).

The Christian life is a decision and it is one that is not going to please everyone. And that is as it should be. Christianity, if we do it right, is going to make some people mad!

By deciding for Christ, we decide against other things. Those who have decided for those things are going to understandably be opposed to and even angry with us. They will see us as the opposition and, indeed, we are. Be clear about that, brothers and sisters, we are, in some areas, the enemy.

We who have taken the words of Jesus seriously about forgiveness will be seen as the enemy by those who live for revenge and retribution.

We who have dedicated our lives to healing will be seen as the enemy by those who have dedicated their lives to hurting.

We who live for reconciliation will always be seen as the enemy by those who live for estrangement and separation.

We who stand for peace are the enemy of those who stand for enmity and we who have decided for love are the enemies of those who have decided for hate.

It's never easy being the enemy.

It's natural to desire the approval and affection of those around us. We all want to be liked. But Jesus calls us to a life that holds other things as more valuable than the approval of authority figures and peers. Some things, he said in Luke's gospel, are more important than even parental approval.

When I was living as a teenager at home, my parents would

recite the same litany every time I left the house: "Have fun and be careful." They wanted me to enjoy my life, but they also wanted me to not put myself in harm's way. It caused them no end of worry and vexation when I decided as a sophomore in college to drop out of school for six months and go to Chicago to live and work in an inner-city reclamation project. They did not forbid it, but they made it clear that it was not what they wanted for me. Yet, as much as I wanted to please my parents, I felt called by God to do that work even if meant facing their disapproval.

Now, as a parent and grandparent, I find myself on the other side of the same dilemma. I didn't necessarily want my children to become firefighters, but neither would it have broken my heart had they decided to become bankers, teachers, or civil servants in some nice, quiet, safe little suburb. When my son spent the year before going to graduate school, working with mentally ill people who sometimes became violent and my daughter chose that same year to work in an inner-city church, I was proud of them, of course. But I would have slept a little better if I thought they were safer. But what could I do? If that was where God was calling them to serve, and they both insisted that it was, who was I to intervene?

We all tell our kids to be careful when they leave home. Yet we know that it is likely that sometime, God will call them to do that which is not careful, that which is not safe, that which is not popular. God sometimes calls us to do that which our parents would frown upon.

And not just parents, either.

As United Methodist Bishop and former Duke University Chaplain William Willimon rightly said, we live in the post-Christian era of American history. No longer does the church and synagogue determine the normative morals and values of our society. Popular culture and pseudo-scientific, pop psychology have taken up the task and we have gladly turned it over to them. The result is what US News columnist John Leo described as a society that clings to traditional virtues such as honesty, loyalty, and commitment but only in principle. In practice, we treat them as personal options that we can accept or reject at our convenience. "Honesty and commitment are all well and good," the culture tells us, "Unless they get in the way of our personal goals and desires, at which point they can be cast aside as unrealistic and unbearable burdens." (US News, August 12, 2001.)

In a culture such as this, those who stand for any absolute will inevitably be seen as freaks. Those who stand for unconditional love of family, total commitment in marriage, undiluted honesty in commerce, utter loyalty in the workplace, will be derided as naïfs at best and, at worst, fools.

When a recent survey of college students uncovered that a larger percentage than anyone would have guessed had lied and/or cheated on their college entrance tests and applications, a radio reporter was sent out to get the responses of college students. The interviewer asked some anonymous kids on an Ivy League campus if they had cheated or lied on their entrance exams and applications. All three admitted that they had. What about honesty, the interviewer asked. Isn't honesty important? You could almost see the kids rolling their eyes. Yes, they agreed, honesty is important. But this was college! This could affect their entire lives.

Their entire lives, indeed.

Good News, Bad News

The gospel lesson teaches us that there is both good news and bad news.

The good news is that God has weighed us and judged us, and by the grace and love of Jesus Christ, has found us acceptable. The Creator of all that is desires for us to come and sit at a banquet table that has been prepared for us and be God's adopted sons and daughters.

The Lord of history requests the pleasure of your company.

And the bad news is that just as sure as we say yes to that kingdom, that family, that life to which God has called us, we're going to end up making somebody mad.

But only if we do it right. Amen.

Proper 16

Luke 13:10-17

No Excuse

> But the leader of the synagogue, indignant because Jesus had cured on the sabbath, kept saying to the crowd, "There are six days on which work ought to be done; come on those days and be cured, and not on the sabbath day."
> Luke 13:14

When my brother, Brian's kids were little, he used to coach football. Well, coaching may be too strong a word. These were nine and ten-year-olds and Brian used to say that what the league called coaching was really more like herding cats.

The team practiced twice a week where their two coaches taught them the fundamentals of football: blocking, tackling, throwing, and catching a pass, that kind of thing.

Then they would play a game on Saturday morning where they all forgot or refused to remember the fundamentals they had learned and just ran around the field like a swarm of locusts. Brian's son, Jake, was a big, tough kid for his age, with a talent for blocking, and Brian said that, basically, the team had three plays that sometimes worked: 1) Quarterback run behind Jake; 2) Running back run behind Jake; and 3) Punt.

Brian said that he spent a lot of their practice time teaching and making sure the kids stayed hydrated. And they scrimmaged a lot because they loved playing the game more than they loved learning about it. Brian tried to make the practices fun because nine-year-olds have a less than perfect understanding of delayed gratification. Their idea of delayed gratification was something like having to wait in line for an ice cream cone.

More than anything, he said, he wanted them to have the

experience of working together as a team to overcome the difficulties of a tough, demanding enterprise, even if that enterprise was only a game. He wanted them working together to overcome problems, in other words.

One of the problems they had to overcome was wind sprints, an often grueling series of all-out dashes, one after another, designed to build up an athlete's strength and lung capacity. The fact that wind sprints are a good idea, however, didn't make it easier to get the kids to do them.

At the end of each practice and after each game the coaches would call the team to the end of the field and say, "Okay, boys, line up for wind sprints." At that very moment, several of the boys would develop heretofore undiscovered injuries to keep them from running. They would come limping over to the coaches, or they would come walking, holding one part of their body or another, grimacing and groaning, declaring that they had, just that moment, discovered a debilitating, even crippling injury that could very well prove fatal if aggravated by the brutal punishment of even a single wind sprint.

On one particular Thursday evening, at the end of the practice, the coaches called the boys to the end of the field, as usual, and, as usual, seven or eight of them lined up in front of Brian limping or cradling their injuries. One by one, they went down the line, bewailing their manifest misery, each one, oddly enough, having a different one than the one before.

When they finally came to the last boy, he looked up at my 6'7", 270 pound brother and grabbed his right arm, thought for a moment, then grabbed his left arm, thought again, grabbed his thigh, then his knee. Finally, Brian stopped him. "What's the matter, Dale?" he asked. "Can't remember where you were injured this evening?"

Brian and his friend, the other coach could not help but laugh and, good sports that they were, the other, "injured" boys laughed and, finally, Dale laughed as well.

Then they all ran their wind sprints.

In relating this story to me, Brian pronounced a benediction on the whole affair: "If they had spent half the time and energy studying the game and getting in condition that they spent thinking of excuses, we could have won the Super Bowl."

Excuses: A Biblical Perspective

In this day's gospel lesson, Luke related the story of Jesus healing a woman who had been bent over for eighteen years by something like scoliosis or osteoporosis.

It was the sabbath and Jesus was teaching in the synagogue, when the woman entered. Scholars tell us that, since only men would have been sitting at the table doing Bible study with Jesus, she was probably there for a women's class or personal, private prayer, or she might have been a cleaning lady.

Jesus saw her and, without a moment's hesitation, he pronounced her healed and touched her. The pain left her, she stood up straight, and she began praising God.

But all are not happy at this outcome. There are some legalists in the group, who care more about rules and regulations than they care about relieving human suffering, more about doing things right than about doing right things. Their spokesperson, the chairman of the administrative council, voiced the group's indignation.

"Hey," he said, slamming down his Bible. "Healing is considered work and there are six days in the week for working. This is the sabbath when we are supposed to rest from work. She would still be crippled tomorrow, you know, and you could have just as easily waited until then to heal her and that's what you should have done."

Jesus isn't about to be lectured on church rules by this crotchety old curmudgeon. No running in church. No loud talking in church. No short pants in church. And now, no healing on the sabbath. For crying out loud!

He called them out: "The torah allows, and any one of you would allow as well, that, if your ox or your donkey was thirsty on the sabbath, it would be allowable for you to work enough to untie the animal and lead it to the watering trough for a drink."

Everyone nodded their heads. They all knew that this was so.

"And yet," Jesus went on, "This woman, this member of your church, was not just thirsty or uncomfortable. She had been suffering and, not for just an afternoon but for eighteen years, but you would make her suffer for 24 more hours rather than break some obscure, esoteric, outdated church rule. What a bunch of hypocrites you are."

His point was hard to miss, here, wasn't it? You worship a God who tells you to love your neighbor as yourself, but you love the law more than her so you use it as your excuse. The fact is, you would rather let her suffer when you could just as easily have helped her.

And, once again, his opponents were put to shame and the crowd sang his praises. The leaders of the synagogue who were called to show mercy, compassion, and love were better at making excuses than they were at hearing and heeding God's call.

I'm glad that happened two thousand years ago, aren't you? If it had happened today, it might have been really uncomfortable.

But then, it still is happening today.

To what is God calling us? To what task? To what ministry? To what endeavor? And what are the excuses we use to put off that call so we don't have to do things we really just don't want to do? I wonder if the answers to those questions are really all that different, today, than they were 2,000 years ago when the synagogue's administrative council members were making up their excuses.

Excuses We Uses

The stories in the Bible continue to address our lives thousands of years after they were first written down because they speak to our experience. Whether we accept them as literal, historical fact or metaphor and myth, the stories ring true to us. We have had the experiences of which they speak.

We all want a Moses to lead us out of our distresses but, when we get one, we complain that he isn't leading us fast enough or in the way we want to go.

We want a leader, a king, to tell us what to do but we complain when Saul turned out to be human like the rest of us.

We all want prophets to tell us the will of God. And we all make excuses to explain why we can't possibly heed and follow God's law. Making excuses is just part of what it means to be human and we are as human in our spiritual life as we are in any other aspect of living.

Business consultant James M. Bleech of Jacksonville, Florida, surveyed 110 executives to find out what excuses they hear most often from their employees. Here are the top ten answers:

10. No one showed me how;
9. I was going to do it later;
8. My supervisor doesn't understand;
7. I had too many interruptions;
6. I didn't know it was my job;
5. We've never done it that way before;
4. I didn't have time;
3. Something came up;
2. It was _____'s fault; and
1. It's not my fault.

Notice how none of the employees ever said, "It didn't need to be done." They all conceded that the unaccomplished task was a necessary one that needed to be done. They just didn't do it, but they had several excellent excuses. If this is the way people behave in their professional lives, where their livelihood is on the line, can we really expect them to act differently in their spiritual life?

Inspired by Bleech's work, I once asked a group of clergy friends of mine to write down the excuses they hear most often when people decline to do things at or for the church. The answers will not surprise anyone who has been in a church for more than a couple of years. You may even be intimately familiar with a couple of them. The top ten, in no particular order, were: I'm too busy; I'm too old; I'm too young; I'm too tired; I've never done it before; I've done it too much; it's someone else's turn; I can't work with him (or her); I'll do it some other time (when my kids are older, when I retire, and so on); and, my all-time favorite — *I don't want to.*

Rarely in the church do people suggest that the job we are asking them to do is not worth doing or unimportant. Rarely do they say that the job shouldn't be done. I've never heard someone tell me that teaching Sunday school is a stupid, ridiculous, silly thing that no one should be doing. Nearly everyone will agree that Sunday school is important and someone ought to be teaching or leading it. Just not me - because I'm too busy, I'm too old, I'm too inexperienced, I'm too tired, I've never done it before, I've done it too much, it's someone else's turn to do it, I can't work with that age group, or *I... just... don't... want... to.*

And that's Christian people — non-Christians, unchurched people don't make excuses. They just don't care. It's the people of God who realize that God's will is important. It's the people of God who have to scramble to find excuses for not doing it. And it runs deeper than just doing church work.

Scripture tells us that what God really requires of us runs deeper than teaching Sunday school and showing up on Sunday morning for worship services. What God asks of us reaches beyond our billfold and our personal calendar into the very depth of our soul and the source of our spirit and has to do with our relationship with the ever-present Lord as God comes to us in Jesus Christ.

It has to do with how that relationship is lived out in our relationships with other people. It has to do with gentleness, kindness, and humility, as well as our love and support for each other. Do you think that this may not be the case? Ask the biblical writers and over and over their answers were nearly identical:

Micah: "He has told you, O man, what is good; And what does the Lord require of you but to do justice, to love kindness, and to walk humbly with your God? (6:8).

Isaiah: "Remove the evil of your deeds from my sight. Cease to do evil. Learn to do good; seek justice, reprove the ruthless, defend the orphan, plead for the widow" (Isaiah 1:16-17).

Jeremiah: "Amend your ways and your deeds...practice justice between a man and his neighbor; do not oppress the alien in your land, nor the orphan, nor the widow, and do not shed innocent blood nor walk after other gods" (Jeremiah 7:3 ff).

John the Baptist: "Whoever has two coats must share with anyone who has none; and whoever has food must do likewise" (Luke 3:11).

Paul: "...lead a life worthy of the calling to which you have been called, with all humility and gentleness with patience, bearing with one another in love, making every effort to maintain the unity of the Spirit and the bond of peace" (Ephesians 4: 1ff).

And Jesus: "The time is fulfilled, and the kingdom of God has come near; repent and believe in the good news" (Mark 1:15).

God asks us to change, to turn our lives over to God's will. And yet, we make excuses for our inability to do so: It's the way I was raised. It's the community I live in. I can't help the way I feel. I'm just that kind of person. I'm afraid.

But, if we listen, God is here to answer us even as God answered the young Jeremiah, who was only a teenager when God called him to be a prophet.

I'll Go With You

Recall, if you will, the first chapter of the book of Jeremiah wherein young Jeremiah was called by God through a dream. "I created you for one purpose," said the Lord,"to be a prophet to the nations."

Jeremiah, no doubt still rubbing the sleep from his eyes, was ready with an excuse why he couldn't possibly do as the Lord asked: "Ah, Lord God! Truly I do not know how to speak, for I am just a kid."

But God stopped him in his tracks.

Don't say I'm just a kid. Don't say I'm too young. Don't make any excuses.

God does not want excuses. God wants results, and a thousand excuses, no matter how good they are, do not make up for a single good result.

But he does not leave us with that, like some despotic boss who threatens that if you can't do the job, he'll find someone who can. He's not going to abandon us to a job for which we are not equipped or prepared. He is not going to make demands and then walk away, leaving us with a task that we cannot do. Listen to how he responds to Jeremiah:

"Do not say, 'I am only a boy'; for you shall go to all to whom I send you, and you shall speak whatever I command you. Do not be afraid of them, for I am with you to deliver you, says the Lord" (Jeremiah 1:6-7).

You see, the promise of scripture is that we do not need excuses because we have God.

God will go with us. God will give us the knowledge, the ability, the wisdom, the experience we need if only we will answer God's call and bow to God's will. God will go with us and deliver us from every insecurity and distress — whether God sends us to a children's Sunday school class, a church choir, the chairmanship of a committee, a hospital room as a visitor, or a youth group as a counselor.

Whether God calls us to the front line of a protest, the desk of a difficult career, a community that is different than any we've ever lived in, or a totally new direction for our lives, the promise is the same.

And that promise is nothing less than the great and eternal truth that God does not call those who are prepared. God prepares those who are called, if only they will not let their excuses get in the way. Amen.

www.ingramcontent.com/pod-product-compliance
Lightning Source LLC
LaVergne TN
LVHW091000080826
845145LV00003B/1074